Twayne's United States Authors Series

EDITOR OF THIS VOLUME

Sylvia E. Bowman

Indiana University

Willard Motley

TUSAS 302

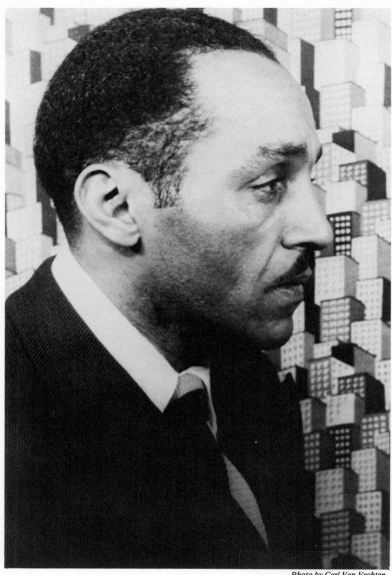

Willard Motley

WILLARD MOTLEY

By ROBERT E. FLEMING

University of New Mexico

TWAYNE PUBLISHERS
A DIVISION OF G. K. HALL & CO., BOSTON

Library of Congress Cataloging in Publication Data
Fleming, Robert E.
  Willard Motley.

  (Twayne's United States authors series ; TUSAS 302)
  Bibliography: p. 161–65
  Includes index.
  1. Motley, Willard, 1912–1965 — Criticism and interpretation.
PS3563.0888Z6   813'.5'4   77–25308
ISBN 0–8057–7207–3

To my mother and father

Contents

About the Author

Robert E. Fleming first became interested in Willard Motley while completing his doctoral dissertation on the Chicago Naturalistic novel at the University of Illinois. He is professor of English at the University of New Mexico, where he teaches in the American literature and American studies programs. He is also the author of *James Weldon Johnson and Arna Wendell Bontemps: A Reference Guide,* published by G. K. Hall.

His essays on nineteenth and twentieth century American literature, most about the works of Afro-American novelists, have appeared in a wide variety of professional journals, including *American Literature, Arizona Quarterly, Contemporary Literature, CLA Journal, Negro American Literature Forum, Negro History Bulletin, Phylon, Studies in Black Literature,* and *Mid America.*

Preface

Willard Motley's claim to a lasting place in American literary history seemed assured in the years immediately following the publication of his best known novel, *Knock on Any Door* (1947). In addition to selling well, Motley's first book became an artifact of popular culture, inspiring a *Look* magazine picture story, a King Features comic strip, and a movie starring Humphrey Bogart. Early reviewers did not hesitate to compare the new author to Theodore Dreiser, James T. Farrell, and Richard Wright, and they sometimes did so to the distinct advantage of the newcomer.

After his initial success, Motley worked hard to improve his mastery of the craft he had chosen and to prove that he was not simply a one book novelist. Hence, there is bitter irony in the fact that his reputation declined steadily during the 1950s and 1960s even though — or perhaps because — he continued to attempt new techniques and to explore new subject matter in three more massive novels. Because of his consistent use of white protagonists, even the belated but increasing recognition accorded Afro-American literature since the late 1960s failed to reawaken interest in Motley. Only very recently has a growing group of scholars begun to reexamine Motley's work critically and to edit his correspondence and journals, which shed additional light on the life and work of this latter-day Naturalist.

In the first chapter of this book, I have traced the diverse nature of the influences that made Motley the kind of writer he became — his race, his precocity as a writer, and his growing awareness of society's ills during the Great Depression of the 1930s — and I have discussed his early nonfiction and his first experiments in fiction. Each of his four novels is discussed in a separate chapter which examines Motley's literary objectives, his view of society and its treatment of the urban poor, his methods of handling the themes he chose to use, and his literary theories. Throughout, I have attempted to integrate the familiar view of Motley as a social critic with a fresh consideration of the author as a literary artist. Chapter 6 details some of Motley's later projects, which might have appeared in print had it not been for his early death. Finally, I have attempted to assess Motley's achievements as a novelist writing in the dying mode of Naturalism, as an Afro-American who wrote sympathetically of white characters, and as a critic of society's dehumanizing influences.

For making available papers from the Estate of Willard Motley, I wish to thank Mrs. Frederica Westbrooke, executor, and Walter Roth, attorney. Special thanks are also due to Jerome Klinkowitz and Kathleen Hinton, who generously made their edition of Motley's diaries available to me before publication, and to James R. Giles and Jill Looman Weyant, who helped me to find my way through the extensive collection of letters, manuscripts, clippings, and holograph diaries in the Swen Franklin Parson Library at Northern Illinois University. I also thank Robert Fisher and Felix Pollak, librarians in charge of the Motley collections at Northern Illinois University and the University of Wisconsin, respectively.

For financial support, I am indebted to the Research Allocations Committee of the University of New Mexico. Finally, and most important, I am grateful to my wife Esther for her help in editing, typing, and proofreading and for the support and encouragement she gave me throughout this entire project.

ROBERT E. FLEMING

University of New Mexico

Acknowledgments

I wish to thank the following for permission to quote from the works listed:

"The Almost White Boy." Copyright © 1963 by Willard Motley. Quoted by permission of McIntosh, McKee and Dodds, Inc.

Knock on Any Door. Copyright © 1947 by Willard Motley. *We Fished All Night.* Copyright © 1951 by Willard Motley. Quoted by permission of Hawthorn Books, Inc.

Let No Man Write My Epitaph. Copyright © 1958 by Willard Motley. Quoted by permission of Random House, Inc.

Let Noon Be Fair. Copyright © 1966 by G. P. Putnam's Sons. Quoted by permission of G. P. Putnam's Sons.

Excerpts from "The Diaries of Willard Motley," "The Beer Drinkers," and "Little Sicily" are quoted with the permission of the Estate of Willard Motley. No part of these stories may be reproduced in any form without permission in writing from Walter Roth, attorney for the Motley Estate (D'Ancona, Pflaum, Wyatt, and Riskind, 30 North LaSalle Street, Chicago, Illinois 60602).

Chronology

syndicated newspaper comic strip condensation of the novel. *Knock on Any Door* is condensed in *Omnibook* and is the subject of an eleven-page picture spread in *Look*.

1951   Publication of *We Fished All Night*. Moves to Mexico.

1958   Publication of *Let No Man Write My Epitaph*.

1960   Addresses Athenaean Literary Society, University of Wisconsin.

1965   March 4, dies of intestinal gangrene in Mexico.

1966   *Let Noon Be Fair* published posthumously.

CHAPTER 1

A Long Apprenticeship

F EW authors have written so convincingly and movingly about the slums of large cities and about the problems of the lower classes as has Willard Motley. And yet, contrary to the impression given by many capsule biographies — an impression that Motley may sometimes have fostered deliberately — he himself was by no means a product of the slums. Rather, Motley was born and reared in a middle class environment quite different from the settings of his novels, and he was not to leave his bourgeois home until, during his twenties, he was impelled by a feeling of rebellion against his own world and by a desire to search for more interesting materials for his writing.

I *Family Background*

Willard Francis Motley was born in Chicago, Illinois, on July 14, 1909, although he was later to give 1912 as the year of his birth.[1] His father, Archibald Motley, Sr., was a Pullman porter on the "Wolverine," a train running between Chicago and New York City. When Willard was growing up, Mary (Mae) Motley, his mother, was perhaps the strongest influence on him, but he was also undoubtedly influenced by the artistic example of his brother, Archibald, Jr., who was even then a successful painter, a noteworthy achievement for a black man in that period. Between Willard and Archibald came a sister, Florence, who was known as Flossie to the family.

The Motleys were the only black family in the South Side Chicago neighborhood where they first rented an apartment and where they later bought a house at 350 West 60th Street. Willard was "born in a private white hospital and two weeks later baptized in the [Roman Catholic] cathedral," facts that he later cited to show the degree of acceptance enjoyed by his family.[2] In these early years of the twentieth century, before the expansion of Chicago's black belt, white neighbors apparently felt little threatened by the presence of a single black family. Willard's recollections of the neighborhood, with its mixture of German and Irish families, were mostly pleasant, although in the 1960s he wrote of one incident that suggests that all was not harmonious between the races:

My father had been respectfully invited to a meeting by several business-men of the neighborhood. They were very polite. Friendly. Cigars were passed around. They told him what they wanted.

He came home storming.

There had been the usual talk of "property values." They had invited him to "join the club." He would sign with them their "ungentlemanly agreement" not to rent or sell to Negroes or Jews.

"Why, Mae!" he said, "I wouldn't be able to sell or leave our home to my own brother!"

And, in angry dignity, not considered a part of a Pullman porter, he had walked out on their meeting.[3]

Willard also remembered hearing the terms "kike," "polack," "dago," "greaser," and even "nigger" in this relatively quiet area of Chicago; on the other hand, he remembered an aunt who visited his parents reluctantly and asked his mother, "How can you live around all these old white people after all they did to our people?"[4] When Willard moved into the slums of Chicago to get closer to his material, he contrasted the democratic attitude he found in the "worst" areas of the city with the stuffy prejudices of the middle class neighborhood.

In spite of these negative incidents, Mae Motley taught young Willard by both precept and example the principle on which he was to insist throughout his life: "People are just people." This prin-ciple, consistently employed by the adult Motley in his fiction, was put to a severe test in 1919 when a major race riot erupted in Chicago. Years later Motley recalled white people who were murderous and others who restrained them:

I was a boy and didn't understand why my father had me piling rocks up in the hall by the front door. The curtain was down, and he stood behind the door with a rifle. If memory serves correctly, next to him, also with a rifle, stood his white neighbor and friend.

The mob came — perhaps 50 or more. A woman neighbor from a block and a half down the street stopped them and, wagging her finger under the leader's nose, said, "Don't you dare bother that colored family down the street or you're going to have trouble with all of us." Their answer: "No, we're going to the West Side to get some niggers."

As they approached our house, the woman across the street ran out, telling them the same thing. They walked past our house without looking at it. Late that night my cousin came panting and coatless into the back door, a bullet through the brim of his hat, which he somehow still held in his hand. He had been caught between the Negro and the white districts on his way home. My father silently motioned him to a place in the hallway for the long night's vigil: We live or we die here in our house. Not as a victim but as another American defending his right to be here.[5]

Looking at both the hostile whites and those who defended his family, Willard chose to accept the positive side of the white race. Throughout his life, he was to speak out sharply against black spokesmen, particularly the creative writers, who returned hate for hate.

II   *Alias Bud Billiken*

Willard, who embarked on his writing career at the age of thirteen, had surprising success with his contributions to two local newspapers, the Chicago *Defender* and the *Evening Post*. The boy had wanted to become a writer for a year or two before he had anything published; he framed the first dollar he earned by his writing and put his publications in a scrapbook significantly decorated with a picture that clearly showed the race of author Alexandre Dumas, Père. Thus, Willard, who rejected racial hatred from an early age, was not immune to feelings of racial pride; however, his adoption of Dumas as an early hero foreshadowed his own later choice of "raceless" subject matter.

The *Evening Post* contributions are not particularly noteworthy; the young Willard followed standard formats of features normally carried by the "Boys and Girls Post," the children's page. One column was *Dollar Ideas,* first person accounts of how children earned money; and Willard obligingly supplied to it frequent accounts of holding rummage sales, cleaning basements, and performing other chores. Another feature was *The Weekly Short Story,* an unfinished tale for which readers were to supply an ending. Motley's clipping book from the period contains several printed conclusions he wrote, but ironically he was always a runner-up, never a prize winner. A third column, *Clever Pets,* printed a romantic "boy saves dog-dog saves boy" story contributed by Motley. The usual pay for these brief items, as Motley recalled it in the 1940s, was a dollar or two tickets to a downtown movie theater.

The pieces Motley wrote for the *Defender* show a greater complexity and variety. According to his scrapbooks, Willard's first published short story, "Sister and Brother," was printed in three parts on September 23 and 30 and October 7, 1922. Written when he was thirteen, the two-thousand-word story is a romantic account of two orphans taken into the home of an aunt and uncle where they lead a Cinderella style life as poor relatives:

Mrs. Berton motioned the butler to come there. When he came, Mrs. Berton whispered some orders in his ear.

The butler then took Elmer's suitcase that had remained in the hall and led the way up the stairs to a small dingy room in the back of the house. "This is your room, children," said the butler. After he left Elmer looked around the room and said in a disappointed tone, "I expected to stay in a room like Mrs. Berton stays in."

The room contained two chairs of cheap wood not at all like the ones in the living room, one large bed with a blanket that was torn and dirty and one sheet to lay on. In the corner was a washstand.[6]

The story, different as it is from Motley's mature work, is interestingly similar to an experience of Nellie Watkins in his *Let No Man Write My Epitaph.* Publication of the story, bearing his by-line and picture, encouraged Willard to continue working with the *Defender.*

In December 1922, Willard became the editor of a weekly column on the children's page, the *Defender Junior.* The column, entitled "Bud Says," carried both Willard's name and his pen name, Bud Billiken, under a photo of Willard in an editor's green eyeshade and oversized glasses. Intended to appeal to readers between eight and fifteen, the column attempted to generate interest by sponsoring Billiken Club chapters in different neighborhoods and by calling for contributions of drawings, poems, and letters. Willard worked at this job from December 9, 1922, until July 5, 1924; he turned out a column each week, answered letters from readers, and sent birthday cards to members of the Billiken Club. Earning three dollars a week, Willard was surely one of the youngest professional writers in American literary history.

While most of Willard's early columns are of no intrinsic interest, he occasionally broke through the strictures of the childish format to show the kind of writer he was to become. The column for March 10, 1923, is an account of a trip to the Art Institute, where his brother Archibald had two paintings in an exhibition. Cataloguing some of the other painters and paintings, Willard interrupts this rather lifeless recital to describe one of the paintings that most impressed him, Hans Larwinan's "The Bread Line":

This picture shows a line of poor and hungry people waiting in the bread line for food. A little girl about three years old is pictured with a cup in her hand and her mouth is open. It seems to form these words, "Mother, I am hungry." Mothers, fathers, old and young, daughters and sons are shown all waiting for their only food. One poor old crippled man with a pair of glasses on is dressed in rags from head to foot, and the artist has even pictured hunger in his eyes, in fact you can see hunger in all of their eyes. One little boy of our Race is also in the bread line. The whole picture brings to your heart a feeling for the starving in the foreign countries.[7]

Even at the age of thirteen, Willard seemed keenly aware of the tragic lives led by people outside the comfortable middle class niche that his parents had attained. His social consciousness and empathy with the proletarian class, foreshadowed in this early column, were to characterize his mature work; for they influenced his purpose, his choice of subjects, his attitudes, and his development of Naturalistic rather than Romantic tendencies in his techniques.

Three points should be made about these early quasi-literary successes. First, they confirmed Willard in his precocious decision to become a writer by giving him considerable recognition for a boy just entering his teens. Second, his initial successes were in a sense misleading, since he was writing for an unsophisticated audience and for markets in which there was little competition. It must have been uncommonly discouraging for Willard to collect rejection slips during the early half of the 1930s after having enjoyed a reputation as a child prodigy. Third, young as he was, Willard soon realized that just publishing his work and being paid for it was not enough; his writing had to have some social significance.

III   *False Starts*

After graduating from grammar school, where he was the only black student in his class, Motley attended Englewood High

School. Although far from being a ghetto school, Englewood was less stable than the neighborhood grammar school. In a talk that Motley gave in 1960, he recalled that the school, nearly all white when his brother Archibald had attended it some twenty years before, had become racially mixed by the time he arrived and that many of the black students he met there shared a culture entirely different from that of his own middle class family. "The Negroes, even the girls, were carrying switchblade knives," he remembered.[8]

The school's atmosphere was uncongenial for a small, bookish freshman; nevertheless, he seems to have been happy as a high school student. He was active in extracurricular activities, including football, intramural basketball and baseball, track, the boosters' club, and, more importantly, the school newspaper and yearbook. After his graduation, in January 1929, Motley was so reluctant to leave Englewood that he took a few postgraduate courses and served as a volunteer assistant coach for the football team. Unable to find a job because of the depressed state of the economy, he continued to live with his parents while he pursued his interests in sports and writing. The writing did not go well: Motley, who had spent an uneventful life up to this point, really had nothing more than high school athletic feats to inspire him.

One remedy for a lack of subject matter was to see more of the world. Travel adventures were in vogue in the 1930s, and on July 3, 1930, as he neared his twenty-first birthday, Motley embarked on what was to be the first of several lengthy trips. With fifty-one cents in his pocket, he set out for New York City on a bicycle and arrived there in only thirteen days. On the way, he slept in a jail (voluntarily) in Michigan City, Indiana; in the press box of the South Bend, Indiana, football field; and in the basement of a Catholic church in a small town in Ohio.[9] Although he had not approved of the trip, Willard's father wired ten dollars to his son in Ashland, Ohio. Motley spent a month in New York, drinking in the sights and enjoying a certain amount of adulation for his bicycle trip. This trip whetted Willard's appetite for adventure, but he did not take to the road again for several years.

Instead, he settled himself at his desk and seriously applied himself to the task of becoming a writer, "knocking out these short stories, with the idea that the egg had to become a chicken. The idea of selling to *Saturday Evening Post,* Sports Magazines [*sic*], *Liberty* Magazine, and that sort of thing."[10] These were discouraging years, for Motley lacked the experience necessary to write for the quality magazines to which he was sending his manuscripts. As his list of rejections mounted and he failed to make a sale, his father and his older brother grew certain that he would never become a successful writer and tried to convince him that he was wasting his time. They viewed Willard as a loafer and a dreamer who was simply putting off the time when he would have to settle down and make a living at one of the uninspiring jobs open to "colored" men. Only Mae Motley encouraged him and slipped him money to buy stamps and envelopes.

Incomplete records that Motley kept from this period show that he was submitting stories entitled "Irony," "Leper Woman," "Supreme Sacrifice," and "Lovely Muriel Cohen" to *Esquire, Colliers, Liberty,* the Chicago *Times, Midweek* (published by the Chicago *Daily News*), the New York *Times,* the New York *Daily News,* and *American Magazine.* On his chart, the column that he optimistically reserved for sales remained blank.[11] Although Motley did not retain copies of any of these stories, they were probably like two existing unpublished stories that also seem to date from this period — Romantic tales with the "twist" endings popularized by O. Henry.

"The Homecoming" is about a young hobo who returns to his home. Having run away ten years before, he assumes that his parents will not recognize him as he asks for a handout, and he plans to reveal his identity later. While he eats, the parents tell him about their son who ran away and was killed by a train. Both are glad he died as he did: if he had returned after such a long absence, they would have rejected him because he would probably have been a criminal rather than the good boy they raised. Shocked, the son leaves without identifying himself. Then the conversation between the parents reveals that they knew him immediately, but sent him away because he seemed to be a fine young man while they are now criminals and fear to corrupt him.

In a similarly sentimental story, "November Twenty-Second," a banquet is held on that date to honor a famous doctor for his numerous acts of charity. When the guest of honor fails to arrive, a friend goes to find him and is told about the doctor's mysterious past. His father was a poor newspaper salesman who made great sacrifices to send his son through medical school. Yet, when his father was ill and asked his son to sell papers for him on a snowy night, the doctor refused; his father contracted pneumonia and died. Now every November 22, the anniversary of his father's death, the doctor roams New York selling papers.[12]

One can only concur with the judgments of numerous editors who rejected such amateurish efforts. Discouraging as the repeated rejections must have been, Motley remained determined to become a writer, though it was clear he had a great deal to learn before he could produce fiction worth publishing. In 1941, when Motley looked back to this period, he realized just how naive and romantic he had been.[13]

In 1936, when Motley recognized how unsuccessful his attempts at formula fiction were, he left home on another "hobo trip," this time to the West Coast. Apparently he thought of the trip as an opportunity to gather material because he kept careful notes, some of which he later used to advantage in his writing projects. An early product of this trip was an unpublished manuscript about his experiences during a month in jail in Cheyenne, Wyoming. Having run out of gas and money in subzero weather, Motley approached a Catholic rectory and asked the priest for a loan. Unlike some clergymen Motley had met on his travels, this priest proved to be unsympathetic and refused to help; he turned the young adventurer back into the cold. Motley then attempted to siphon gasoline from a parked car, which he later claimed ironically belonged to the same priest, and was caught by the local police.

According to the article, the experience was not so unpleasant as might be supposed. "In All the World No Trip Like This!" is a romanticized account of Motley's stay in the Laramie County Jail and of the other inmates he encountered there. The tone of this narrative is as different as possible from that of Motley's later accounts of police brutality and of a jail's corrupting influence on the lives of juvenile offenders. The jail was casually run by a young deputy who made a trusty of Willard; and, unlike some of Motley's later criminal characters, his fellow prisoners are presented as interesting personalities, most of whom are in jail for short sentences on such relatively minor charges as fighting, stealing rides on freight trains, or petty theft comparable to Willard's own crime. Little attention is accorded to those convicted of more serious crimes such as embezzlement and rape. All in all, Motley's treatment of lawbreakers is reminiscent of O. Henry's, and the general thesis of the piece is that a jail is a fascinating place to stay for short terms and that people on the inside may be more colorful than people on the outside.[14]

Different as this article is from Motley's later work, it reflects his early sympathy for criminals and his recognition of their positive qualities. On the other hand, the literary technique differs significantly from the objectivity Motley attained in his mature work. The narrator-author is very much a part of the action and strains to convince the reader of his adventurous attitude. For example, he dramatizes the way he kept notes on toilet paper and smuggled them out of the jail in his underwear (this part of the story, at least, is literally true, for the notes are among his papers on loan to Northern Illinois University) because of a rule against keeping journals. Since the lax discipline of the jail as described in the article itself hardly called for such concealment, the general effect is one of Tom Sawyer-like self-aggrandizement. Probably Motley was thinking of pieces like this one when he later noted in his journal his early tendency to be too subjective in his writing.[15] The value of the jail experience itself, however, was considerable. Perhaps more than any other event in his life up to this point, it broke through the respectable middle class shell that Motley's parents had constructed and made it possible for him to learn about the type of life with which virtually all of his successful fiction was to deal.

Another unpublished manuscript deals with more typical aspects of the trip. "Pennies for Passage" tells how Motley and a companion worked their way from Portland, Oregon, to Los Angeles, often driving until Bessie, their dilapidated twelve dollar Buick, ran completely out of gas and they had to coast off the road. At such times, the two men would canvass the town, looking for odd jobs. Their meals were usually pancakes or beans, which Motley cooked over a portable stove beside the car in good weather and inside the car when it rained. Their chief worry was running out of gas in a town too small or too poor to afford them jobs worth a few cents in gas money.

On this trip Motley encountered the first prototype of his most successful fictional character, Nick Romano. Although it was some time before he realized the literary value of this meeting, the experience did impress him emotionally at the time. In 1960 he told the story in these words:

On one of these trips in the city of Denver, I had this old car and enough fuel for me and the car if I washed windows and cut lawns and so forth, and much as it is in the book [*Knock on Any Door*] I was passing this street, when there was this little boy, Mexican boy. . . .

I looked at him and the little boy smiled at me, and I sort of waved at him and he ran up to the fence and smiled at me and he said, "will you talk to me". [sic] He was a boy at that time of about twelve or thirteen..., I don't remember. We talked for a while and I asked him why he was in that reform school or detention school, and I asked him if his mother came to see him, and he said no, and if she did he would just bawl. So I took his address, went to see his mother and told her that the kid was lonesome.[16]

Motley was to see and correspond with this boy and his family for years after this first meeting.

Arriving home in August 1937, Motley attempted to use the material he had been accumulating to write several travel articles. Although he had completed some fifteen articles and sold one by the following summer, he set out on June 30, 1938, for a second western trip which would furnish additional material. This time, instead of trying the "slick" magazines, Motley submitted the articles to less spectacular but more appropriate markets for a beginning writer and thus broke into print for the first time as an adult. His initial sales were to magazines like *The Highway Traveler,* published by Greyhound Bus Lines; *Outdoors,* a sportsman's magazine which paid him in merchandise from an advertiser; *Automobile and Trailer Travel Magazine*; and *The Ohio Motorist,* published by Ohio's branch of the American Automobile Association. The high points of his writing career in the late 1930s were two sales to *The Commonweal.* Some of the pieces, such as "Idaho Presents Shoshone Falls," "Assault on Catalina," and "Calle Olvera — America's Most Picturesque Street," are straight travel articles that have no special bearing on Motley's later work; but they did help to restore his self-confidence and to encourage him in his determination to become a professional writer. Three of the better pieces, however, foreshadow significant elements in his later fiction.

" 'Religion' and the Handout," published in *The Commonweal,* opens with an account of Motley's personal experiences in various mission soup kitchens where he ate during his travels. Motley conveys the moral indignation that was to characterize his fiction as he tells how hungry men are subjected to sermons, which may last as long as two hours, before they are allowed to eat. He remembers in particular an abrasive sign in front of a mission in Los Angeles — "YOU MUST ATTEND THE SERVICES TO EAT HERE" — and recalls that the food was frequently not fit to eat when it finally arrived. In contrast, Motley describes the St. Vincent de Paul Society of Denver with its atypically homelike atmosphere.

Although he arrived after meal time, he was taken to the kitchen and served one of the best meals he had eaten while on the road. Motley's point becomes clear when he tells of returning the next day and eating with the mission's habitués:

> Around the table sat men of all nationalities, of all creeds. A good number were atheists. Side by side sat the hardened road boy, the petty crook, the panhandler, the thief, the honest man out of work, the old criminal out of "stir" again and ready to resume his career, the tough, the smooth-cheeked boy on his first tilt with life, the hitchhiker, the consumptive old man hawking into a dirty rag — the unloved and ungodly.
>
> . . . .
>
> It is amazing what a change came over those men sitting there eating. The hard, pinched look left their faces. The cynical light in their eyes softened to a look of compassion and humility. Sometimes even tears were detected in eyes that had never wept. The edge had been taken off of all the men. Their roughness had been left on blatant Larimer Street. They laughed and conversed in modulated tones. It was always: "Please pass the bread." "Thank you." "Don't you want some more potatoes?" Never the slang or rough words of the street. And no man ever sat at that table with his hat on.[17]

The article is representative of Motley's writing at the time. Although he had discovered the material that was to dominate his works, he still had a boyish tendency to romanticize elements of the lower class and the underworld.

The most significant items in the Motley bibliography for 1938 and 1939 were two articles in *The Ohio Motorist*. "The Boy" is a first person account of his meeting with Joe, the young Mexican American who was the initial inspiration for Nick Romano. Motley seems to present the meeting as it occurred, with little attempt at artistic shaping. The author sees the boy, who is working on the grounds of a Denver detention home, and talks to him, first through the high wire fence and later inside the home after gaining admittance with a fake press card. Convicted of stealing a bike, the thirteen year old boy impresses Motley with his curious mixture of innocence and precocity as a criminal: one moment, Joe talks about crying with despair; in the next, he suggests to his new friend how easy it is to steal twenty to fifty dollars from ice cream trucks. Motley then visits the boy's mother; pays several more visits to the home with candy, fruit, and cookies; and leaves Denver feeling sure that he will never see the boy again. However, in the 1939 sequel,

"The Boy Grows Up," Motley tells of revisiting Joe, who has stolen another bicycle and is in the home again. Noting that Joe has become harder in the past year, Motley becomes more aware of the brutality of the school. He emphasizes the stories he has heard about mistreatment of the boys and tells of the scars he has seen on one little boy's bottom.[18] The parallels between Motley's role in these articles and Grant Holloway's in *Knock on Any Door* are readily apparent and help to explain why Holloway so often seems to be a spokesman or persona for the novelist.

After his second trip to the West, Motley set to work on a book identified by two working titles, "Adventure" and "Adventures and Misadventures." Charles Wood, who has studied the 474 page typed manuscript extensively, describes this unpublished work as

the autobiographical narration of two journeys from Chicago to the west coast, taken between late November of 1936 and the summer of 1938. Structurally, the "plot" of the work is simply chronological, or even geographical. The book is very uneven in that it makes no effort to strike a balance between time and space. Motley devotes long passages to events, people, and places which interested him, and frequently he brushes over long periods of time and great segments of the country when he is interested in getting on to other things.[19]

In spite of his success in producing publishable articles from his travels, Motley was never successful in shaping these travel materials into a finished book.

This unpublished manuscript and the travel articles show Motley leaving behind the attitudes that had influenced his writing in the early part of the 1930s. No longer was he a writer selling a story primarily to make money or to satisfy his own ego. Nor was he the Romantic who was searching for picturesque characters and adventures. In spite of the fact that he signed "The Boy" rather flamboyantly — "Willard F. Motley: Fool, Adventurer, Scribbler" — he had begun to believe that literature should serve a social purpose, should trouble the conscience of its complacent readers.

Motley's new commitment was at odds with his middle class home life, and he left his parents' house for an apartment of his own:

Feeling that I could not write or learn about man in the narrow boundaries of my neighborhood where a Pole was a "polack" and an Italian was a "dago," where no new thoughts were moved in, I moved to the slums of

Chicago. Here I would at least see that people were not all of a pattern. Here I began my first novel.
My friends and their parents feared for this "alien son" of theirs. I was to look out for those people "down there," watch my step: their enemies, their fears rested with the "dagos," "polacks" and "greasers." And here I wandered around at 2 or 3 in the morning "looking for material." No knives, no razors were pulled on me. Friends were made. I found my childhood belief to be true: People were just people.[20]

Motley found a small, dirty apartment at Fourteenth and Union and rented it for twelve dollars a month. It was not a comfortable place to live — Motley said later that the bathroom had a dirt floor and was regularly visited by a resident rat — but, since there were few distractions, Motley found it a good place to work.

While living in this neighborhood, Motley began to visit Hull House at 800 South Halsted Street. Founded by Jane Addams and Ellen Starr in 1889, Hull House had become an intellectual center, especially for young artists with liberal or radical ideas. There he met two men who were important influences on his early career, William P. Schenk and Alexander Saxton. Although Motley had seen more of the world than either Schenk or Saxton, both surpassed him in formal education and in knowledge of literature. Saxton, who was to be a lifelong friend of Motley's, lent him books by John Dos Passos, John Steinbeck, Ernest Hemingway, James Joyce, and Leo Tolstoy. Among Motley's papers is a reading list given to him by Schenk at this time, suggesting works by writers as varied as Carl Sandburg, Steinbeck, Thomas Mann, Homer, Anton Chekhov, Emily Dickinson, Ambrose Bierce, Robert Herrick, Henrik Ibsen, James Weldon Johnson, Sinclair Lewis, Upton Sinclair, Jack London, and Sherwood Anderson. Especially singled out were two works on Chicago, Ben Hecht's *One Thousand and One Afternoons in Chicago* and *Chicago: A History of Its Reputation* by Lewis and Smith. Up to this point Motley's self-discipline had been directed more toward his own writing than toward any sort of systematic reading program, and the suggestions made by Saxton and Schenk provided much-needed guidance. Encouraged to read more widely and to learn more about his craft, Motley found the attractions of Romantic writing fading, and he discovered Realistic ways of putting his varied experiences and acquaintances down on paper.
In the fall of 1939, the three friends founded *Hull-House Maga-*

zine, with Schenk as editor and with Motley and Saxton as associate editors; the three men were also the major contributors to the
new monthly. Although it was modest in format, the first issues
being mimeographed, *Hull-House Magazine* brought out the best
in Motley. Forsaking the paying markets for his travel articles and
the manuscript for his book "Adventure," he began to produce
Realistic, plotless sketches of the neighborhood that are faintly
reminiscent of some of Ben Hecht's newspaper columns. No longer
a casual visitor who would pick up a few colorful details before
passing on to another town, Motley settled down to a closer observation of the life around him. "Hull-House Neighborhood," which
appeared in the first issue of the magazine, describes the area in two
parts, "Asleep" and "Awake." Like an exercise for a creative writing class in its form, the short piece recreates the appearances and
sounds of the neighborhood and attempts to evoke in the reader the
moods that these sensory impressions awaken. Thus, not only was
the quality of his observations improving, but also the artistic shaping of those observations.

"Pavement Portraits," from the second issue of the magazine, is
a more ambitious piece. Motley moves to Maxwell Street, one of
his favorite locations in Chicago, for a study of environment and
character: "This is the corner. Here is where the women stand at
night. This is where the evangelists preach God on Sundays. Here is
where knife-play has written a moment's strange drama; where
sweethearts have met; where drunks have tilted bottles; where
shoppers have bargained; where men have come looking — for
something.... This is the humpty-dumpty neighborhood. Maxwell
and Newberry...." The area itself is a microcosm: "This is a
street of noises, of odors, of colors. This is a small hub around
which a little world revolves. The spokes shoot off into all countries. This is Jerusalem. The journey to Africa is only one block;
from Africa to Mexico one block; from Mexico to Italy two blocks;
from Italy to Greece three blocks...."[21]

Motley moves from the general impressions to specific details as
he describes the street's inhabitants: a group of crapshooters, a
streetwalker, a double amputee who rolls along the street on a dolly
made of boards and roller skates, a fourteen year old Mexican
truck driver, the tramps who raid garbage cans. At times Motley's
old Romantic attitude insinuates itself, as when he treats the streetwalker: "And once I heard this woman of the side-long glance from
the shadow-piled doorway say to another slattern, 'My sister is

coming to see me today. She has a little girl!' Her voice leaped like a heart beat and I turned to look at her.... I had never seen eyes so wondrously lit before. Then something happened inside the woman and there came a second look — I turned and walked down the street so fast that I was almost running away from her.'"[22]

But there are also unmistakable signs of progress in his technique; for example, he sometimes presents a dramatic scene that conveys the poignancy of slum life without overt moralizing on the part of the narrator, as in this brief encounter: "A bum, his foul rags wrapped about him like a cape, halts in front of the hot dog stand on Halsted. Goldie, the good looking but hard Jewish girl behind the counter says, 'Go on, beat it.' — 'Huh?' — 'Do you want something?' — 'Will you give me something?' — 'Yeah — POISON.' "[23] Thus, in spite of occasional lapses, Motley was learning to avoid mawkish sentimentality and emphasis of the merely picturesque, two characteristics of the local color approach to his material in his juvenile writing and in some of his early travel pieces.

In a third contribution to *Hull-House Magazine,* Motley contradicts the common beliefs that people in slum neighborhoods are hard-hearted and immoral. "Handfuls," printed in January 1940, consists of four anecdotes that are connected by the same theme. The first story is about a girl who has lost her mother's last five dollars on Maxwell Street. The people in the crowd, poor as they are, take up a collection and replace the sum with their nickels and dimes. The second sketch is a fragmentary argument between a layman and a sidewalk evangelist about the necessity of loving the drunks and derelicts of the street. Somewhat predictably, it is the layman and not the preacher who recognizes the bums' humanity. The third sketch shows the notion of honor that operates among the inhabitants of Maxwell Street, who will not steal from the open stands and pushcarts although most of the people are always hungry; and the last sketch emphasizes the spirit of brotherhood and fun manifested at a street dance on Newberry Street.

Clearly, Motley intends all four sketches to illustrate his credo that "people are just people" and that the people who live in a slum may be more admirable in some ways than those who live in respectable middle or upper class areas. The fact that the sketches convey these ideas without subjective commentary by the narrator indicates Motley's growing awareness of what he could accomplish through selectivity of details and incidents to dramatize a theme.

Thus, the author seems poised on the border between journalism and fiction.

The experiences afforded him by *Hull-House Magazine* were extremely valuable to Motley at this stage of his career. Although he had finally realized his ambition of becoming a professional author of sorts with his journalistic travel articles, he had had no previous encouragement of his more creative writing. Small as its circulation was, *Hull-House Magazine* offered him the chance to see his works in print and to profit from the reactions and criticism of his fellow editors, Schenk and Saxton. While none of the contributions is of exceptional literary merit, they do show that Motley was learning the techniques of fiction and that he was developing a more mature philosophical concept of the world and of the place of the writer in it. There is a considerable difference between the writer who signed himself "Fool, Adventurer, Scribbler" and the author of the slum sketches.

Motley continued to write in a Realistic vein throughout 1940; however, he had to devote more of his time to earning a living now that he had left home. After a period of drawing relief checks, he worked on a street labor gang (an experience that he was to use in telling Pa Romano's story in *Knock on Any Door*). In April 1940, Motley got a notice to report for work on the Works Progress Administration Writers' Project, which employed him for the next two years. At first a lowly subordinate, he was promoted to professional writer at $96.00 per month, effective July 1, 1940.[24] He found time to write a number of short stories utilizing the new objective, Realistic technique he had begun to develop in the *Hull-House Magazine* sketches. One story written during this period and submitted to a literary magazine brought him to the attention of Jack Conroy, a well-known member of the Chicago literary establishment in the early 1940s.

Some ten years older than Motley, Conroy had also traveled around the country as a bum and an itinerant worker before becoming a writer. He had had even less formal education than Motley when he began his literary career in the late 1920s, contributing to left wing publications, editing anthologies of revolutionary verse, and eventually moving toward respectability as a regular contributor to H. L. Mencken's *American Mercury*. By the time Motley met him, Conroy had published two novels: *The Disinherited* (1933), which had attracted considerable attention; and *A World to Win* (1935), a less successful work. Motley had worked with Conroy in the Writers' Project, but he did not know him well until he submitted a story called "The Beer Drinkers" to *The Anvil,* of which Conroy was editor. Although Conroy rejected the story, partly because of its length, he pronounced it publishable and told Motley that there was no reason why he should not submit it to a more commercial market such as *Esquire.* He asked about Motley's previous publications and his future plans, saying that, if Motley had a novel in progress, he would be glad to introduce him to some of his publishing contacts.[25]

The story that so impressed Conroy and initiated a friendship that was to last until Motley's death was the most polished piece of work that Motley had yet written. Nineteen pages in typescript, the story is a relatively plotless study of Arleen, an upper middle class girl, and her ambivalent attitudes toward Bill, her proletarian lover. The story opens with an "accidental" meeting on the street, planned by Arleen to try to win Bill back, and tells about their love affair in a series of flashbacks. Arleen had picked Bill up in a bar and had begun the affair, which Bill had eventually broken off. Arleen is eager to resume the relationship, but is willing to settle for friendship with Bill if that is all that he can offer her. In the part of the story that takes place in the present, Arleen invites Bill to her apartment, ostensibly for a beer and a friendly talk; and the two make love. But Bill tells Arleen that he is in love with a girl from his social and economic class and leaves the impression that he will never be back.

Thematically, the story expresses the conclusion toward which Motley had been moving during the 1930s: it is in the lower class, with all its apparent rough edges, that the true warmth and vigor of life are to be found in the modern world. Arleen has had other working class lovers before Bill, as well as lovers who were intellectuals, artists, and socialites. She has lost Bill because she cannot accept him completely and give him a love that is genuine. Moreover, she has fed on his tough masculinity while keeping him at a distance and still maintaining close ties with men whom she can respect intellectually.

Arleen's ambivalence toward her former lover is evident early in the story:

She watched, almost fearfully, and a shivering moved along her skin. Her lips opened a little and sucked in a sharp breath of air as, for a moment, she stood without movement on the sidewalk. He was coming

noiselessly, quickly, out of the canyon of the long street. And inside of her
two urges worked like hands in biscuit dough. Could she turn and walk the
other way, *fast, fast, faster?* Run! She wanted to. But she couldn't.

She had walked these streets for two months faithfully — hoping to
meet him supposedly by accident. Now that he was here, she felt that she
couldn't face the impact of a meeting with him. This coarse, animal of a
man. This vulgar factory hand. This laborer![26]

In spite of the contempt that she sometimes feels for him — and for
herself because she cannot simply forget him — Arleen needs Bill in
a way that he does not need her. After Bill has left her for the last
time, Arleen lies in the bed thinking of her current lover, Kennie,
whose very name suggests immaturity and boyishness: "She
remembered his slimness, his soft blond hair and the surprising
dark eyes beneath. And she drew away, into the bed, from the
memory. She was tired out. Body and mind. But she couldn't sleep.
She didn't want to sleep. All she wanted was to shut the door on
Kennie and to call up, lazily, all that had been hers and Bill's; and
more recently all that had passed between them that night. And her
nose, in the pillow, searched for him."[27] Lower class strength, bred
in the hard everyday struggle to earn a living, triumphs over the
effete class that spends its time in the pursuit of pleasure.

"The Beer Drinkers" shows strengths that Motley had not previously exhibited. The writing is carefully done, suggesting that he
had spent more time rewriting than had been his early practice. By
focusing primarily on two characters, he had forced himself to
probe more deeply into the psychology of his creations. The dia-
logue is realistic and unaffected, and the settings are economically
but effectively sketched, without Motley's earlier tendency toward
local color picturesqueness. Altogether, the story provides conclu-
sive evidence that Motley had come of age as a writer.

Other good Realistic stories that date from this period were never
published. "Father Burnett's Vestry" explores the relationships of
a priest with three members of his parish: a twelve year old boy, an
eleven year old girl, and a woman who has marital problems. While
Father Burnett is drawn to each of the three sexually, he says or
does nothing improper; and the story is a delicately handled study
of the lonely nature of the priesthood contrasted with the life of the
outside world; for, although each of the three is troubled, all experience life more fully than their confessor. The physical side of sexual maladjustment is treated in "Needles," the story of Dorothy
Jamison, a thirty-six year old housewife who is bored with mar-

riage. She has a casual affair with a lamp salesman and then happily goes back to her dull husband Hubert. Dorothy feels good at the conclusion of the story because she has briefly escaped the safe middle class world in which she lives.

"Niño de la Noche" is more experimental than any of the other stories. This plotless character study focuses on Carlos, a young Mexican American, who drinks wine and smokes marijuana while he thinks about his past. Although he is still quite young, he has had a wife and son, from whom he is now separated. He thinks of them and then about his boyhood as the son of a migrant worker in Texas. He recalls how his sister died of tuberculosis and how he recovered with no medical aid but folk medicine. Motley handles the story well; he avoids the pitfall of excessive sentimentality and achieves the same sort of effect that one finds in F. Scott Fitzgerald's "Babylon Revisited" or in Ernest Hemingway's "Snows of Kilimanjaro" because the essence of the main character's life is distilled into a brief retrospective moment.

Several stories written during this period are interesting in their treatment of racial conflict, a topic that Motley normally avoided altogether or at least deemphasized. A long untitled story tells of a day in the life of James McLean, the middle-aged foreman in a railroad roundhouse. Frustrated by his son's unwillingness to go to law school, by his wife's nagging about a new house, and by his own failure to advance at work, McLean focuses all his bitterness on Richard Israel, a black worker. Balked in his attempt to fire Israel, McLean goads him into a fight; and Israel reluctantly beats him up. McLean is now able to fire Israel for cause, but he returns home that night full of the same frustration that had plagued him that morning.

A second well-developed story dealing with race is "The Almost White Boy," which remained unpublished until long after Motley had achieved recognition as a best-selling novelist. This story of Jim Warner, son of a white father and a black mother, begins with Motley's favorite assertion that people are not to be judged by race or nationality. However, much as Jim wants to believe in the principle taught him by his father when he was a very small boy, he continually encounters people who judge him racially rather than personally. Because of his gray eyes and blond hair, black children with whom he grew up teased him with the epithet "white nigger" and his own aunt told him he looked like "poor white trash."

The plot concerns Jim's love for Cora, a white girl from a

bigoted family. When Jim tells her on their first date that he is a Negro, he notes a change in her manner although she continues to date him. When they discuss race, Cora suggests that Jim is silly not to pass for white; and his reply that people are just people, that his race should be acknowledged but not given undue importance, begins to sound hollow even to Jim. Nevertheless, the two young people attempt to carry on a conventional courtship. Each goes to dinner at the home of the other with rather awkward results. Ultimately, Cora offers herself to Jim sexually and he rejects her offer, saying that he wants to marry her. Cora angrily runs away from him after calling him "nigger"; and Jim, left alone, repeats his father's precept as if it were an incantation: "When she was gone he lay on his face where he had been sitting. He lay full length. The grass he had pulled stuck to his lips. 'People are just people.' He said it aloud. 'People are just people.' And he laughed, hoarsely, hollowly. . . . Then it was only a half-laugh with a sob cutting into it. And he was crying, with his arms flung up wildly above his head, with his face pushed into the grass trying to stop the sound of his crying."[28]

Technically, the story is less impressive than "The Beer Drinkers," but it shares the polish of the other stories written during this period. The chief fault of "The Almost White Boy" is that Motley relies too heavily on straight narration and fails to dramatize as effectively as he might in the first half of the story. Attempting to cover Jim's life from his earliest recollections to the time he meets Cora is an artistic mistake that Motley might have avoided by the use of flashbacks, a technique he employs with good results in "The Beer Drinkers" and "Niño de la Noche."

However, as an index of his thinking at the time, the story is important for two reasons. Motley's journals from the 1930s tell the story of his love for Theresa Mulligan, a white girl who became a close friend and who might have become more had it not been for race. Although Motley's relationship with Theresa's father was good, there was enough awkwardness to stimulate Motley's imagination. Nevertheless, the strain of racial bitterness that runs through the story is an unusual note for Motley. The fact that the same note also appears in several unpublished stories and fragments written at about the same time suggests that he may have been tempted to abandon his conviction that an artist should speak to and for all races. Once embarked on his first novel, however, Motley reaffirmed his decision to become a "raceless" writer.

On the whole, most of the finished stories from this period show sufficient professional skill to account for the confidence that friends like Saxton and Conroy had in Motley's eventual success as a writer. His experiences during the 1930s and his exposure to academically trained fellow writers had tempered the excessive Romanticism so characteristic of the younger Motley.

Supporting the evidence of these short stories is Motley's journal entry for January 1, 1941. He wrote that he had "grown up" artistically, and that he had made a "jump from the subjective to the objective both in thought and in my writing."[29] However, "subjective" and "objective" may not have been the precise terms for what Motley meant to convey, for he added that "some authors write at a great distance from their subjects, some very close to their subject. I want to write as a part of my subject."[30] On July 14 of the same year, his thirty-second birthday, he further stated, "I want my character[s] to be human, fallible but likeable. I don't want to pass judgement on them and don't want my readers to when they finish with them."[31]

What did Motley mean by these seemingly contradictory statements? Clearly, he did not rule out sympathy with his major characters; rather, his objectivity seems one-sided: he refused to condemn the actions of the character. At the same time, he rejected as subjective the intrusions of a narrator who can be equated with the author himself, as in "The Boy." Viewed in conjunction with the stories he was writing at the time, the statements also seem to rule out the excessive sentimentality that had flawed some of his early efforts. Another important change in his fiction, although he does not specifically mention it in the journal, is his rejection of the contrived and often melodramatic surprise ending in favor of the type of low key, seemingly inconsequential ending that Hemingway had popularized in his short stories during the 1920s. Motley had at last reached the point where he was capable of writing a successful novel.

CHAPTER 2

Knock on Any Door

C ONTRASTED with the small projects that had occupied Motley during the 1930s, the composition and revision of his first
novel occupied most of his time for nearly seven years. Nothing in
his previous experience had really prepared him for such a monu-
mental task. But the book was also to meet with popular and critical success that was far beyond the author's most optimistic
expectations.

I *The Writing of* Knock on Any Door

In the January 1, 1941, entry in his journal, Motley recorded the
fact that he had completed three chapters of his first novel, under
the working title "Leave Without Illusions." Based on the same
young Mexican American who had inspired "The Boy" and "The
Boy Grows Up," the novel was intended to have a double thrust, as
Motley explained in another journal entry a few months later. The
reader was expected to leave the book stripped of his illusions
about reform schools, the police, and the effects of the urban environment; and Nick Romano was to lose his illusions about the
world around him before being executed for murder.[1] In an early
note, Motley listed the "villains" of the book as being the Denver
reform school and its superintendent; the Chicago juvenile detention home; the police; West Madison, Maxwell, and Halsted streets
as well as the slums in general. Finally, he planned to show that the
breakdown of the social system that included the police, the family,
and the neighborhood shared the blame for Nick's character.[2]
Thus, Nick's personal tragedy would have broad social implications that might educate others.

Motley's journal and personal papers from this time reflect a
curious combination of objective and subjective attitudes: his
investigation into the background material of the book was thor-

36

ough and sometimes almost clinical; but, in his relationships with the real people on whom the characters are based, he often evidenced a deep personal commitment. As early as 1938, Motley had written to the Colorado State Industrial School in Golden requesting that Joe, the first prototype of Nick Romano, be paroled in his custody. Motley assumed that if Joe were removed from his Denver neighborhood and acquaintances, it would be possible for him to stay out of trouble. The request was not granted; and, when Joe was paroled, he was sent back to his parents' home. Motley kept in touch with Joe indirectly by corresponding with his mother, and in May 1941 he received a letter telling him that Tino (Joe) was on his way to Chicago: he had stolen two suits, and the Denver police were looking for him.

Tino stayed with Motley for some two months; he found a job and encouraged Motley to think that he might be able to save his young friend from a life of crime. "If I can straighten Tino out and give him a break," Motley wrote in his journal, "really see that he gets started right it would be doing more than writing books that were best sellers and lived after I am gone."[3] As long as Tino was working, he seemed cheerful and happy, insisting that his benefactor take most of his paycheck to pay for their expenses; but the job soon bored him and he quit. Finally he told Motley that he had decided to return to Denver and plead guilty to the theft charge, clearing his account with the law. Later Motley found out that Tino had not done so; he had gone with his brother to Los Angeles, where Motley lost track of him.

During this same general period, Motley, following the methods established by earlier literary Naturalists, went to great lengths to insure complete accuracy. He conducted research of various kinds, from sitting in homosexual bars to visiting reformatories and courtrooms. In a February journal entry he tells of going to "the Bench" on Clark Street to find a real man to identify with the homosexual Owen, who was beginning to take shape in his mind: "I know how 'Owen' looks — his mouth, eyes, hair; but I know nothing else about him, where he works, where he lives, what his life before meeting 'Nick' was like. Think maybe if I look around and listen around long enough I'll eventually see someone who might be like 'Owen.' "[4] He also spent a lot of time sitting in a cheap cafeteria at West Madison and Halsted, "getting the feel" of the restaurant that was to become the Nickel Plate in *Knock on Any Door*.[5]

The painstaking research he did over a period of so many years is evident in his emphasis on concrete details, whether in his specific use of street names and his description of bars, restaurants, and alleys or in more arcane subjects such as the exact grip favored by jackrollers or the mechanical intricacies of the electric chair. The entire setting of the novel is precisely drawn, a tribute to Motley's careful note taking and his supplementary use of the camera.

As part of his research, he went in April with Alexander Saxton to St. Charles, Illinois, to visit the State Industrial School for Boys. One boy of about eighteen reminded Motley of the character who was becoming Nick Romano. Like Grant Holloway in his own novel, Motley responded to a request for a cigarette by dropping several on the ground out of sight of the guards. Another project, which Motley began in the fall of 1941, was learning firsthand about courtroom procedure. When September brought a murder trial that seemed made to order for his purposes, Motley recorded, "Sawicki is a youth, 19, who murdered four people, one a policeman. In court he is hard boiled and cocky — a pose of course. Have been taking notes at the trial and will use some of the material in my novel. Talked to Sawicki's lawyer, Mr. Morton Anderson, assistant public defender, and after the trial he is going to have me come and see him and discuss Sawicki and the trial with me."[6] In October, when Motley went to see Anderson, he found the lawyer helpful and described him as being "on the side of the poor, oppressed, young."[7] Anderson, who approved of what the writer was attempting to do in his novel, answered his questions on how a defense case was set up, invited him to come back for more advice if he needed it, and gave him permission to use part of his closing argument from the Sawicki case in the novel.

Another important influence on the book that was taking shape was a young criminal named Mike, whom Motley had first met in 1940. In his journal Motley stated that, while he had had Joe in mind when he was writing the Denver chapters of "Leave Without Illusions," Mike was the model for Nick from the time the Romano family moved to Chicago and Nick began to be affected by the West Madison Street neighborhood. Mike had already served an apprenticeship in minor crimes such as jackrolling and burglary, but Motley characteristically refused to believe that Mike was truly bad and soon befriended him, as he had earlier tried to help Joe. He visited Mike in the Cook County Jail, fed him at his apartment, gave him liquor, and lent him money. In October 1941, Motley's generosity backfired when he allowed Mike to borrow a suit and left the key to his apartment hidden so that Mike could return the suit. When Motley got home later that night, his camera and typewriter were gone and there were no signs of forcible entry. Correctly assuming that Mike was guilty, Motley sent him a note by a mutual friend. The items were returned, but Mike avoided Motley for some time.

Although shaken and temporarily embittered by Mike's treachery, Motley soon regained his faith in human nature and in Mike: "I had encountered a 'boy criminal's' vicious instincts; and I had found the 'boy criminal' just a boy — neither good nor bad. A boy. And I liked Mike and go on believing in him."[8] Five months later the incident was forgotten by both when Mike came to Motley's apartment to hide from the police. The association came to an end after Mike was sentenced to prison on July 31, 1942; ironically, he had not committed this crime. Motley recorded in his journal that Mike had been caught with two sixteen year old burglars who had just robbed a house. Because of his bad record, no one believed that Mike was innocent, and he was given a one to five year sentence, while the other boys were given probation because of their youth. Motley wrote "The Beautiful Boy," a short story about Mike, and submitted it to the *Atlantic Monthly,* but it was never published. He later incorporated most of it into *Knock on Any Door,* where it formed the basis for Chapter 44 in which Grant Holloway takes Nick to the Wisconsin woods on a camping trip.

One of Motley's Works Progress Administration projects dovetailed nicely with his work on the novel. In March 1941, he was assigned to do a study of living conditions in the "Little Sicily" section of Chicago. Having recently become interested in photography, Motley created a presentation combining pictures, captions, and text on life in the Italian neighborhood where slum tenements were being replaced by public housing sponsored by the Chicago Housing Authority. Although buildings were being demolished and new apartments were being constructed, the residents of the neighborhood still endured the same squalid living conditions. Motley chose to stress the misery of the residents and the toughness of their children rather than the dubious hope held out to them by the new housing projects. A typical picture shows a boys' crap game, and Motley's caption reads:

Crap Shooters

"Little Sicily" was first known as "Little Hell." "Little Sicily" has a

reputation for being *tough*. It has its "Death Corner" where there have
been more than half a hundred killings. It is here, encompassing the
Cabrini Home site, where juvenile delinquency rates are highest in the city.
The photograph shows a group of young boys "shooting craps" behind
the St. Philip Benizi school (see brick wall).[9]

Working in this neighborhood, Motley became familiar with Italian
customs and made acquaintances who were to be useful in round-
ing out the characters of members of Nick Romano's family. He
also familiarized himself with the speech patterns of Italian Americans. Finally, he saw daily a confirmation of the thesis that his
book was designed to illustrate — the death of innocence in such an
environment.

By the beginning of 1942, Nick Romano had become more real
to Motley than many of the people whom he encountered in his
everyday life. On February 8 he had a birthday party for Nick,
complete with a birthday cake topped with sixteen candles. A note
in the journal states that this is Nick's real sixteenth birthday; his
fictional birthday is August 27. Apparently February 8 was the
birthday of Nick's first model, Joe. Eight months later, when Motley recorded the writing of the scene in which Nick kills Officer
Riley, he wrote almost apologetically in the margin of the journal,
"What could I do? Nick would have acted as he did. I stood
observing — and wrote down what I observed."[10] The feeling that
Nick was almost a real person extended to Nick's wife Emma as
well. Motley became quite depressed when the time came for Emma
to commit suicide. But the most difficult scene to write was Nick's
execution. In April 1943, although Motley was looking forward to
finishing the novel and submitting it to a publisher, he wrote regret-
fully, "This weekend or next I have to kill Nick. It is not a pleasant
thing to look forward to after three years of living with him, know-
ing him better than I've ever known anyone and — liking him."[11]

In spite of his deep personal feelings about the story he was writing, Motley avoided his earlier fault of excessive sentimentality by
continuing to emphasize his scientific approach. In March 1942, he
took the chapter in which Nick is sentenced to a Chicago judge and
asked him to read it and check it for accuracy. A year later, in
preparation for the task of writing about Nick's execution, he made
an appointment to see the warden of the county jail. Although the
warden helpfully provided the necessary information about how
the electric chair worked and how executions were conducted, the

interview was a brutal emotional experience, as Motley noted: "Still feel like puking from his discourse on the efficiency of the chair, the record of only six seconds to strap a man in and start the juice burning through him, his wall of 25 photographs of the men who have died in the chair since he has been warden — these photos being in his office on one side of his desk where he can see them."[12] Motley left the interview feeling that he would like to "really tie into" the warden; but when he actually wrote the execution chapter, he settled for making the warden a mild hypocrite who tells a reporter, "I make it as easy for my boys as I can."[13]

Finally on June 1, 1943, having delayed the execution as long as he could, Motley killed Nick, writing the last chapter of the novel with tears in his eyes. He then immediately wrote the first few pages of another novel that he had been contemplating, for he felt that he could thus overcome the twofold depression he had experienced at ending not only the life of his favorite character but also the book on which he had worked for almost three years. The new book, which he called "Of Night, Perchance of Death," furnished poor therapy; he ended the night by going out to get drunk.

But the first book was far from finished. All during the summer of 1943 Motley was busy revising the last part of "Leave Without Illusions" and retyping the manuscript. Finally, on September 16, he packed the novel, 1951 pages, into a wooden box and sent it to Harpers. On November 3, the novel came back, rejected. Motley had been so sure of the worth of the book that he was inordinately depressed; he alternately felt that he really couldn't write and vowed that he would show the editors at Harpers how good he was by becoming a success. He felt so little confidence that he could not resubmit the novel for some time, but in January 1944, he sent it to Macmillan's, where he had better luck. The letter that arrived on March 12, 1944, expressed interest and asked Motley to make extensive revisions and resubmit the manuscript. Motley seems to have held out for a definite commitment, for on April 6, 1944, Macmillan gave him a firm contract and a small cash advance, both of which were welcome. Motley's Works Progress Administration project had been terminated, and he had been supporting himself by working in an animal surgery laboratory at the University of Chicago and later in a Thompson's restaurant as a fry cook.

The publishing house stipulated that Motley revise the manuscript to suit them, chiefly by cutting the length to two hundred fifty thousand words. Mary S. Thompson, a reader for Macmillan,

suggested that some of the long conversations and descriptive passages be cut to achieve the desired length, but she praised the work
profusely. Macmillan expressed two other objections to the novel:
it dealt frankly with sex, especially the taboo subject of homo-
sexuality; and it named actual taverns and other Chicago business
places that might conceivably sue for libel. Although Motley had
considered his first novel finished and was hard at work on his second, for which he hoped to receive a Newberry Fellowship, he
turned once again to "Leave Without Illusions." By 1946, he had
completed two full revisions, only to have Macmillan reject the
novel on the grounds that there was still too much sex in it and that
the revised version seemed to lack the power of his original
manuscript.

Meanwhile, Motley had been awarded a Newberry Fellowship on
the assumption that he was working full time on his second novel.
Bitterly disappointed at this setback, he sent the final, revised
manuscript to Appleton-Century. This publisher accepted the novel
immediately and offered the author an advance without quibbling.
Only the title displeased Appleton; Motley suggested as an alternative a line that he had used on the first and last pages of the novel;
Appleton approved and *Knock on Any Door* was at last complete.
In later years, Motley exaggerated the number of rejections he had
experienced before finding a publisher. However, in 1947 he told
Ray Brennan, of the Chicago *Daily Times,* the outline of the story
given above, which is substantiated by his diaries.[14]

II   *The Principles Underlying* Knock on Any Door

Early in 1947, before the publication of his first novel, Motley
wrote a preface for the book. Although Appleton decided not to
publish it, Motley kept the preface in his files. The essay offers insights into Motley's intentions in *Knock on Any Door,* his practices
as a novelist, and his growth as a writer during the previous seven
years. Motley began by admitting that he didn't know whether he
had written a "good" book or a "bad" book. All he knew was that
he had been as honest as possible in telling the story of Nick
Romano. He had not attempted to make the book "artistic" in any
self-conscious way because "the author's style, his language, his
idiom, should be that of his characters...."[15] He deliberately
attempted to submerge his own personality — a wise decision
considering the sentimentality in some of his early work — because

he felt that "the author is of minor importance and should be a lay-figure in the hands of his characters rather than the other way around; that the author doesn't belong on a pedestal looking down at his characters — however sympathetically."[16] He had tried to get into Nick's mind and present the world as Nick saw it, and he wanted to be judged primarily on the accuracy of the presentation.

Motley discussed the character of Nick Romano and its origin in two real boys he knew and in his "conception of a third." This last, rather enigmatic remark may be partially illuminated by Motley's assertion at the end of the preface that he knew "at least twenty" potential Nicks living within a mile of his apartment. Emma, he said, was based on the early life of a friend; and most of the minor characters were also based on real people he had known. The plot was his, but he insisted that the reader must accept the reality of the characters, events, and environment. He feared that some readers might consider the book mere entertainment and dismiss it as "just fiction." It was important to Motley that the reader should be educated and influenced by the book long after he had read it.

Motley's concern about the reader's reactions has its roots in his concept of the role of the creative writer. He asks the rhetorical questions, "Of what use is the writer to society? Isn't he, too, just a parasite?"[17] The answer, for Motley, is that the writer must come down from his ivory tower and live the life of the common people. Those writers of his period that he most admired had done so, and Motley himself had done so since leaving home. Such a writer cannot help identifying himself with his fellow man:

The writer, today, sees himself in these other people and these men and women in him. And if he is honest, first as a man and secondly as a writer, he cannot but write about them and against the things that oppress and injure his fellow man. In other words the writer approaches his subject matter — his fellow man — in humility and understanding, in sympathy and identification — but without glorification. And he tries — only the serious writer knows how hard — to tell the truth, frankly and unshrinkingly.[18]

Such a writer must necessarily spend a great deal of time exposing what is wrong with the world, "tearing away ... one more brick of the phoney structure" and "helping in the making of a new world." Motley was aware that this type of writer would make fewer friends among his readers than would the entertainer and that his work might be called propaganda rather than art, but he responded, "If this type of writing is propaganda then the modern

writer is a propagandist; if this be 'inartistic' then art, 'pure art'
has always been a parasitic growth scratching at the surface of life
and reality and receiving board and keep from patrons whom it was
desirable to please and flatter in exchange for the delight of being a
fat and self-pleased parasite in an ivory tower.''[19]

Realistic writing is ugly, Motley admits, but it is ugly only
because life is ugly for the people whom the writing describes.
People who say that they are depressed by Realistic literature are
attempting to escape the ugliness of reality, and they ask that the
writer divert them from unpleasant matters. The serious modern
writer, says Motley, refuses to be drawn into such an arrangement.
Instead, he puts "the pavement and the cobblestones and the sweat
and blood and tears of real people on paper.''[20] This is what Motley
has attempted to do in *Knock on Any Door*: to interpret the dangerous young men like Nick Romano and the tough neighborhoods
that shape them so that the more comfortable sectors of the American population might see them — perhaps for the first time.

III   *Live Fast, Die Young*

Knock on Any Door introduces Nick Romano as a young, innocent boy. His parents, solid middle class Italian Americans, hope
that their altar boy son will be a priest. However, with the second
chapter of the novel, the fortunes of the Romano family turn
downward; their food store fails, and they move to a poor section
of Denver. Nick attends a new school and is exposed to boys like
Tony, who teaches him to mock the nuns and to steal apples and
pies. When a friend of Tony's forces Nick to hide a stolen bicycle,
Nick is sent to reform school for stealing it.

The reform school warps Nick's personality. There the boys are
beaten for such relatively minor infractions as not getting out of
bed as soon as the wake-up whistle sounds, and more ingenious and
sadistic punishments are frequently employed. Hardened older
boys are allowed to terrorize the younger boys by extorting money
and food from them and, Motley hints, by subjecting them to
homosexual attacks. Two experiences turn fourteen year old Nick
permanently against the law and its representatives: one friend is
brutally beaten for attempting to escape and another dies because
of maltreatment. For the first time, Nick finds himself angry
enough to murder as he fights Bricktop, the leader of an inmate
gang.

At the institution Nick first meets Grant Holloway, a writer, and tells him the true nature of the reform school — how the experienced boys teach the younger ones to be more efficient in breaking the law. Later, Holloway meets the Romano family and gives them advice about getting Nick released early.

The Romanos have moved to Chicago to find work and to separate Nick from his old environment, but, ironically, Nick is pleased because he identifies the city with Al Capone. However, he dislikes the new Catholic school that his mother hopes will keep him out of trouble. He roams the rough polyglot neighborhood around Maxwell and Halsted streets with his new friends; he learns from them about sex and the finer points of theft, and he eventually seduces Rosemary, one of the nicer girls in his class. Caught shooting craps in school, Nick is sent to Forman, a school for incorrigible boys, where he develops his ability to fight. He also learns various profitable skills from his friend Vito — how to hotwire cars and how to rob drunks and homosexuals. His old dislike of legal authority, developed in the Denver reform school, is reinforced by plainclothes detectives who shake down petty crooks in the neighborhood and by Riley, a tough policeman who brags of having killed three men.

By the time Grant Holloway encounters Nick again, the boy has become a young criminal whose motto is "Live fast, die young and have a good-looking corpse" (157). Shocked by the change, Grant tries to reform Nick by taking him on a camping vacation in northern Wisconsin, away from the influences that have corrupted him; but the experiment fails, and Nick returns to his old life. Owen, a homosexual who falls in love with Nick, also tries unsuccessfully to keep him out of trouble. Picked up by Riley after a mugging, Nick is badly beaten before the police discover that he is just sixteen and send him to the adolescent home. Back on the street, he buys a gun and vows that Riley will never arrest him again.

For two years Nick drifts, committing petty crimes to support himself, but untouched by the genuine underworld of Chicago. Then one night when he has left his gun at Owen's apartment, Riley catches him and throws him in jail. Correctly suspecting that Riley plans to send him to prison on a false rap, Nick goes for help to Ace, who runs a gambling house in back of a tavern. Through his connections, Ace gets the case dismissed and then hires Nick to keep an eye on big winners, to follow them when they leave, and to roll them for their winnings.

Happy with his new role on the fringe of organized crime, Nick ironically finds himself falling in love with Emma, the type of nice girl who has never interested him since his seduction of Rosemary. In a lengthy digression from the main plot, Motley traces Emma's life from childhood to the time when her first boyfriend was accidentally killed by a drunken policeman. After an idyllic courtship, Nick and Emma are married; Nick breaks with Ace and looks for an honest job for the first time in his life. Over the next month or two, Nick works in a steel mill, a foundry, a factory, and a bakery before he gives up in disgust and goes back to Ace for his old job.

Meanwhile his personal life is in a state of turmoil. His brother Julian, whom Nick has always despised for his honesty and industry, marries Nick's old girl Rosemary. At about the same time, Nick becomes impotent with Emma, partly because he feels unmanned by not being able to hold a job while she works to support both of them. Seeking proof of his virility, he turns to the whores and B-girls he had known before his marriage. When his old friend Vito returns from a two year jail sentence, Nick joins him in a series of "El" station robberies; he again proves his manhood to himself by defying the law. When the two men are caught, Nick, at the age of twenty, is sentenced to a year in the county jail.

Out of jail, Nick takes another factory job and tries to regain his self-respect. Still impotent with Emma, he suffers the additional humiliation of learning that Julian and Rosemary have had a son while he was in jail. Nick tries to explain to Emma that he does not feel good enough for her and confesses his sexual experiences with both men and women. In a fit of depression, Emma gasses herself while Nick is at work, and Nick feels that he has killed her. After a lengthy period of drunkenness, he returns to work for Ace, who moves him into more important and dangerous jobs — delivering drugs and bribes. Courting danger, Nick also freelances in petty crimes.

The climax of the novel occurs when Nick robs a tavern and is chased down an alley by his old enemy Riley. Although wounded, Nick kills Riley, shooting him repeatedly until his gun is empty. In scenes reminiscent of Richard Wright's *Native Son,* the net closes around Nick until he is caught on a rooftop. The police beat Nick to force a confession, but Nick holds out.

Grant hires Andrew Morton, a leading Chicago lawyer, for Nick's defense as the newspapers sensationalize the case of "Pretty Boy" Romano. The trial features various theatricals such as the

prosecution's display of Officer Riley's bloody uniform jacket.
Several of Nick's friends perjure themselves in a vain attempt to
save him. As the trial nears its end, Nick takes the stand, for Morton hopes that Nick's boyish good looks and his innocent air will
influence the jury. Nick holds up well under prosecutor Kerman's
tough cross-examination, but he cracks when he is questioned
about his wife's suicide. Overcome with remorse for his treatment
of Emma, Nick declares that he killed Riley.

Morton tries to salvage the case by telling the jury that Nick was
reacting emotionally when he confessed, and in his summation he
accuses society of making Nick what he is; but the jury returns a
verdict of guilty and Nick is sentenced to die. Morton carries an
appeal all the way to the state supreme court, but he is unable to
save his client. At the age of twenty-one, Nick Romano dies in the
electric chair.

IV   *Sociology and Art*

Viewed from one perspective, *Knock on Any Door* is not unlike a
sociological case study.[21] Motley's semiscientific investigation into
the slums of Chicago led him to emphasize the warping influence of
major cities, which are often difficult places in which to grow up,
especially for the poor. In crowded urban areas, young children
serve an apprenticeship in petty crime and delinquent behavior as
they are tutored by their older and tougher peers. Wholesome
recreational facilities for the young are limited, and the children of
the city develop their own games, which often consist of daring
assaults on the authority of society. Schools tend to be crowded,
and teachers become brutal after years of fighting antisocial young-
sters. Moreover, large city populations offer innumerable victims
and allow the young delinquent to retreat into the anonymity of a
crowd or into the sanctuary of his home area. Living in Denver and
Chicago provides Nick with every opportunity to become a delinquent once his motives are strong enough.

Nick has considerable motivation to stray from the teachings of
his parents and his religion. The elder Romanos, while apparently
not first generation immigrants, are extremely old-fashioned in
their way of life; and, as a child, Nick accepts their standards. He
happily concurs in their expectation that he should become an altar
boy and later a priest, for the Catholic parish in their solid middle
class neighborhood is a sympathetic institution, for a kindly pastor

and admirable nuns are in charge of the school.

When Pa Romano's business goes bankrupt, the stable way of life changes just at the time when Nick, about to enter his teens, is most susceptible to unwholesome influences. The family's move to a different and poorer neighborhood places Nick in a peer group with which he must prove himself in new terms — by showing that he is tough, daring, and able to take harsh punishment without flinching. Parents with an Old World orientation are ridiculed by his new schoolmates, who go their own way and ignore their parents' wishes. In the Romano household, Pa has lost his faith in the American Dream, for he has fallen in a short time from the respected position of small store owner to the lowly position of a man unable to find a job or support his family. Forced to accept money from Aunt Rosa, his sister-in-law, Pa spends most of his time in his bedroom, hiding his shame from his wife and children. For all practical purposes, he has abdicated and left Nick without a father just at the time when the boy needs a strong male figure to admire. Moreover, Pa Romano loses his own belief in traditional values just when Nick is questioning the values that have been instilled in him during his first twelve years.

The church and the school also fail Nick. Unlike Father O'Neill in his old parish, Father Scott is a stern man who does not extend any human kindness to the young people of his parish. Instead, they see him most often as the major disciplinarian of the parish school, where he metes out beatings when the nuns can no longer control their charges. Faced with intractable students year after year, the sisters have become cynical about human nature and treat their students harshly. The boys with whom Nick soon becomes acquainted retaliate with truancy and continual misbehavior in the classroom.

But if family, church, and school are unwilling or unable to educate Nick, other forces willingly take up the task. Boys who are his own age but more knowledgeable about survival are always happy to teach a more innocent member of their group. Nick is befriended by a series of mentors, each of whom he eventually surpasses; as Nick learns more about crime, he in turn passes his knowledge on to younger boys. In the new school, Tony teaches Nick how to steal from bakeries and produce trucks. In reform school, Rocky teaches him how to survive the attacks of guards and other inmates. And in Chicago, Vito teaches Nick how to jackroll drunks and how to commit armed robbery. Unfavorable adult models are always pres-

ent, too, from the Denver pimp who offers to buy a stolen watch
from Nick and his friends to the fence who sells sixteen year old
Nick the gun he later uses to kill Riley.

Society's response to young men like Nick Romano is to meet
force with force, to impose ever harsher punishments for successive
infractions. This generalization holds true from Nick's first beating
in a parochial elementary school, through various reformatories
and jails, to his death in the electric chair. Motley shows how nuns,
priests, police officers, guards, and prison wardens all practice brutality in the name of correction. As a young boy, Nick stole because
he was hungry and misbehaved to gain the approval of other boys
in his gang, but he learns in reform school to hate society, and
crime becomes a way of striking back at the law and the structure it
protects.

While the novel is an effective study of the influence of a poor
urban environment on a weak youth, *Knock on Any Door* is much
more than just a sociological treatise: it is another powerful document in the long-established literary tradition of Naturalism. By the
time the reader has finished the first few chapters, he realizes that
Motley is following writers such as Frank Norris, Theodore
Dreiser, and James T. Farrell in emphasizing character disintegration in a universe ruled by determinism. From the beginning of the
second chapter, which starts with the sentence "Then they were
poor," Nick Romano is in the grip of forces beyond his control as
he struggles to survive in a world he never made. The Naturalistic
novel, with its steady accretion of details and its inexorable movement toward the destruction of the protagonist, transcends the raw
facts on which it is based and moves its readers as statistics and
sociological studies cannot. The strength of *Knock on Any Door* is
Motley's application of the Naturalistic method to a firmly realized, sympathetic main character.

If Motley's study of the urban environment and its corrupting influences sometimes resembles a sociological text, his depiction of
the novel's main character demonstrates the genuine artistry of
which he had become capable. Presented first as a guileless youth,
Nick goes through a number of stages on his way to becoming a
murderer without ever completely losing the basic innocence that is
established in the opening chapter of the novel. When he was a very
small boy, Nick rescued a trapped mouse from a cat that had been
toying with it. Motley uses the mouse as one of his recurring symbols, but on the most basic level, the incident characterizes a boy

who cannot bear to witness cruelty in any form.

Another noteworthy trait in the early Nick is his admiration for the other members of his family, especially his brother. Julian, just a few years older than Nick, overcomes the same influences that send Nick to the death house, but only because he is more mature when the family suffers its reverses. Since Julian's character has been formed during a favorable period, he is able to retain his faith that, through hard work and education, he can lift himself out of the poverty in which the Romanos have become mired. As Nick becomes hardened by his experiences, he grows farther and farther apart from Julian; he regards him as stupid for working hard, saving his money, and attempting to make a place for himself in society on its own terms.

When Nick is plunged into the hostile environment of the new school, he is shocked and frightened by the other students, who talk tough, fight among themselves, and appear uncouth and barbaric to his sheltered sensibilities. His principal reason for becoming a follower of Tony is Tony's ability to fight back against his surroundings. Although Nick does steal at this early stage, Motley makes it quite clear that he steals food because he never gets enough to eat at home. Punishment comes, not for the petty thefts he commits to feed himself, but for things he has not done: first, he is beaten by Father Scott when he takes the blame for a classroom prank Tony committed, and then he is sent to reform school when he hides a stolen bicycle for a friend of Tony's.[22] In this case, Motley deliberately altered the facts he reported in his nonfiction article, "The Boy," in which the young reform school inmate admits that he stole the bike himself. The effects Motley thus achieves are to increase the reader's sympathy for Nick and to provide him with motivation later: that is, society's overreaction to his first minor transgressions forces Nick into a resentful, rebellious position.

The reform school section of the novel builds the view of society as the shaping force that transforms Nick from a slightly troublesome boy into a juvenile delinquent. Probably no one inside the institution really believes that the boys will be reformed by their experiences there. The gym director, Roy Quinn, admits this belief to the new boys in his orientation talk when he cynically tells them, "The law says you stay here until you're reformed. Oh, yes. You'll be reformed when you get out of here. Oh, yes" (29). He later becomes more specific: "We mix you all up here. The clean and the unclean, the young and the old, the innocent and the guilty.... If

you refuse to work or are really the bad type we handcuff you to a
cell in the basement and shoot the fire hose on you until the water
knocks you out or you decide to behave. That's how we reform
you. Oh, yes" (29–30).

While school authorities deal out harsh punishments for minor
infractions of the rules, older and tougher boys terrorize the
younger ones and operate a protection racket within the school.
Boys who get packages from home have to give most of their con-
tents to Bricktop, the red-headed leader of an inmate gang, or they
face a beating from his gang. The leniency of the guards toward
this junior version of organized crime underscores the hypocrisy of
the law and foreshadows later situations in which the individual
criminal is punished while the syndicates are permitted to operate.

But the major turning point in Nick's early life comes with the
cruel treatment suffered by two of his friends, Tommy and Jesse.
Though much younger than most of the boys, eleven year old
Tommy shows an unbreakable spirit, for he resists equally well the
bullying of the inmate gangs and the harrassment of the guards.
Tommy leads a successful escape in which twenty-two of the youngest boys break out, but when they are recaptured, an example is
made of Tommy: he is publicly punished by a beating that is severe
even according to the custom of the reformatory. While the boys
around him silently witness the beating, Nick alone stands and
curses Fuller, the superintendent of the school. Afterwards Nick
reflects that "he'd never be sorry for anything he ever did
again. . . . He hated the law and everything that had anything to do
with it. Men like Fuller were behind it. He was against them" (60).

Jesse's case reinforces that of Tommy. A thin, possibly tuber-
cular Mexican American, Jesse is due to be released in only three
more days when he and Nick are caught smoking. They are sent to
a "burlap party," a punishment session in which a basement floor
is flooded with cold water and the boys are forced to mop it up with
gunny sacks while kneeling in the water. Jesse contracts pneumonia
and dies after a lingering illness. While most of the boys soon forget Jesse, Nick is to remember him for a long time.

Nick's fight with Bricktop indicates the change in the protagonist
within the first seventy pages of the novel. Once a gentle and somewhat timid boy, Nick is now willing to fight and, if possible, to kill
the leader of the gang over a relatively minor argument. Although
Nick is afraid of what will happen to him in the fight, he is more
afraid of retreating from it — a trait that will be central to his

character for the rest of the novel. After he wins the fight, through a combination of luck and stubbornness, he in turn becomes a bully, fighting at the slightest provocation. Nick has discovered how to achieve status in a world that respects only brute force.

Once in Chicago, Nick's descent into a life of crime accelerates. Some vestiges of innocence still exist: Nick is shocked by a street fight that he sees the first time he walks the sidewalks of the new city, and he is still sexually naive enough to be repelled by the actions of his new classmates in the Chicago schools. However, Nick is tough enough to be expelled in a short time from both a Catholic school and a public one. Stealing has a different function in his life than it had in Denver; he now steals items that can be fenced for money to pay for clothes his family cannot afford and for amusements his parents would not approve. Through his friendship with Vito, he learns how to steal cars, jackroll drunks, and blackmail homosexuals. There are few similarities between the sensitive boy who was sent to reform school and the Chicago jack-roller who beats up drunks so helpless that force is gratuitous.

At about the same time Nick is venturing into this deliberate life of crime, he loses another aspect of his innocence. Daisy, a young street girl who seemed repulsive to Nick at first, takes him behind the school for his sexual initiation. Soon after this, Barney, a tough young man from the neighborhood, takes Nick home and forces him to submit to homosexual relations. At first appalled by both events, Nick soon learns to accept them as he has accepted the idea of theft and violence as a way of life.

Sentences in a juvenile home and the county jail complete the process begun by the Denver reform school. Although Nick never loses his disarmingly innocent appearance and can still be curiously vulnerable, as, for example, in his relationship with Emma, he has been damaged beyond reclamation. He comes out of jail a potential killer, ready for his final meeting with Riley.

As Nick moves from "the prayer age" (3) to manhood, he also moves beyond the experience of the average reader, who may find his own sense of morality at odds with that of Nick's crowd and thus feel antagonism for those who flout the accepted principles of society. Therefore, one of Motley's major problems in the characterization of Nick was how to maintain the reader's kindly feeling toward Nick; unless the reader could be carried along by Motley's thesis that Nick was less to blame than society, the novel would fail to achieve Motley's major purpose. Obviously, one device to gain the reader's understanding and compassion was to present each stage of Nick's corruption in great detail, to delineate all the circumstances that led Nick step by step from serving as an altar boy to committing a savage murder.

The main device, however, is similar to that used by James T. Farrell in the Studs Lonigan trilogy: it consists of shifting the focus or point of view of the narrator. While much of the novel is written from the point of view of the omniscient infallible narrator, Motley frequently moves into the minds of various characters, most often Nick's, to decrease the emotional distance between the reader and the character. To some extent, this shift in point of view helps to allay the rather scientific approach so characteristic of Naturalism, but more importantly, it enables the reader to identify more closely with a character for whom he might otherwise have little sympathy.

In an early chapter, for example, instead of Motley's telling us that Nick's mother made him feel embarrassed and uncomfortable, he shows us: "And Ma would say, 'To think you used to be an altar boy! I'm ashamed to own you for my son.' Tears would spout on Ma's cheeks. 'Why do you treat your mother like this?' she'd say. Ma would clutch him, holding him tight against her stiff dark dress with her cheek on his head and the tears falling blop, blop on his hair, making it wet. And he was glad when he could pull away and go outside feeling guilty, kicking at stones and saying, 'Aw, damn it!' " (20). Nick's awareness of the "stiff dark dress" and the "tears falling blop, blop" are direct sensory impressions as they might be perceived by a boy.

Motley's shifts to Nick's consciousness are apparent in his use of Nick's own idiom with many short sentences and relatively simple grammatical constructions, slang, and rather direct descriptions with metaphors or similes limited to those that would occur most naturally to someone like Nick. This passage reflects the consciousness of Nick as a schoolboy: "School started again. But they still goofed around. They had a big fat nun for the last grade. She looked like a scrubwoman with her rough hands and her red chapped face. The guys wouldn't come to school and they'd write each other's absent notes, putting fancy twists to the letters. She never caught on and before September was out they were able to cut class almost half the time" (21). While this narrative technique gives an initial impression of artlessness, it is consciously adopted: this is what Motley means when he writes of the author becoming "a lay-figure in the hands of his characters."[23]

Throughout the novel, then, Motley moves in and out of Nick's mind (and, less often, into the minds of other characters, such as Emma). Thus, the reader shares Nick's reactions as well as his experiences; he may not empathize with Nick completely, but perhaps his moral judgment is suspended or at least less harsh. Early shifts in point of view pave the way for the most effective use of this device in the last two-fifths of the book. After Riley's murder, the reader shares Nick's frantic fear and anxiety:

He started down the gangway. *Dead end!* . . . his mind told him. He staggered forward two steps more and stopped. He stood cornered. His mind whirled. His stomach tightened. *They're going to catch me!* . . . Wildly, obeying mad impulse, he ran out of the gangway and back into the alley. The sheet of rain and roaring thunder followed him. He fled east down the alley. His mind told him No! No! Downtown that way! Run into the arms of the cops! His feet carried him ahead anyway. . . . The raw, cutting air in his lungs choked him. He ran across West Madison. A streetcar clanged and slammed its brakes to keep from hitting him. Lightning beat its hard whiteness against the black sky. The steeple of St. Patrick's Church stood out black in the night. The lightning made him run faster. He was stumbling under a huge beer sign. . . . He ran down the twist of alley behind West Madison. His mind stood up, showing him the Three-Eighty, his own figure backing out of the door onto the sidewalk and Riley yelling "Halt!" *Running in a circle! Back where I started from! Where I pulled the job!* (329)

Only with this method of narration, in which a character seems to give an inside view of his experiences, could Motley hope to have the reader on the side of Morton, Holloway, and Nick during the trial instead of on the conventional side of the prosecution, justice, and law.

While Nick is depicted in careful detail, minor characters are frequently presented rather sketchily. Although Motley usually based even unimportant figures on people he had really known, he often chose an Impressionistic treatment rather than a portrayal in depth. Many times the first thing Nick notes about a character becomes the tag that is repeated at each appearance: a baseball cap with its bill at the rear (Rocky), a chauffeur's cap (Vito), red hair (Bricktop), kinky hair that forms a coxcomb in front (Sunshine), or a phrase like "Hello, pizon" (Holloway). While this technique counters the practice of some Realists and Naturalists, this shorthand method of identifying minor figures suits *Knock on Any Door,* where the focus must remain on Nick on every page.

Impressionistic as they are, Motley's snapshot characterizations are quite effective when he is dealing with the down and out characters he so thoroughly researched. He is less successful with intellectual characters from higher strata of society. For example, the writer Grant Holloway, unlike Motley himself, belongs to a distinctly upper crust milieu. His easy movement between the best society of Chicago, in which his wife's family is prominent, and the bars of West Madison strains the reader's credulity. Although Blanche Gelfant has perhaps exaggerated in calling Grant simply "a sociological commentator and interpreter,"[24] he is one of the least real characters in the novel — a fact all the more surprising because his continuing interest in Nick parallels Motley's own concern for the juveniles upon whom Nick is based.

Another upper class intellectual is Andrew Morton, who becomes Nick's attorney at Grant's urging. Like Grant, Morton is sympathetic toward Nick, and in his closing argument he serves to articulate the wrongs that have been committed against the youth in a way that Nick himself could never believably do. Thus, Morton's function is somewhat similar to that of Boris Max, the lawyer who defends Bigger Thomas in Richard Wright's *Native Son,* but Morton understands his client much better than Max understands Bigger. Both Holloway and Morton are successful in the functions allotted to them in the novel, but they fail to come to life as characters in their own right.

Motley uses several secondary characters to provide perspective on the changes taking place in Nick's personality. Because the narrative technique keeps the reader so close to Nick and because the changes occur so gradually, characters like Aunt Rosa and Grant Holloway are needed to remind the reader how greatly Nick is altered by some of his experiences. The boy who meets Aunt Rosa in Chicago after release from the Denver reform school is very different from the innocent who went there, and although she always accepts him regardless of changes, Rosa bears witness to all the various stages of Nick's decline. Grant, who has known Nick in the reform school, is frankly shocked when he encounters him in a skid row bar and notices how hardened he is.

Motley's conscious art is nowhere more apparent than in his use of symbolism.[25] Several scenes in the novel picture small, relatively helpless creatures who are tortured or killed by relentless forces beyond their control. The most prominent example is the mouse that Nick rescued when he was a small boy. As his mother recalls,

"One day by Rankin's grocery store a cat had a little bit of a mouse cornered and was playing with it — just pawing it and slapping it this way and that. A crowd of people were standing around watching. Do you know what Nick did? You couldn't guess! That child walked up, picked that mouse up and stuck it in his pocket and walked away as fast as he could! If Nick was to die he'd go straight to heaven" (5). Later, Nick himself remembers the incident and adds his own perceptions as he sits trapped by society in the reform school: "the cat didn't have its claws all the way out ... it just patted and slapped the mouse trying to make it run ... trying to have fun with the scared little, black-eyed little, trembling little mouse" (40, elipses Motley's; italics omitted). As his friend Tommy is beaten by Superintendent Fuller, Nick's thoughts return to the mouse; and finally, near the end of the novel, Nick draws a parallel between State's Attorney Kerman's questioning of him and the cat's blows with its partially sheathed claws.

A second recurring image is the death of a young dog, which Nick witnessed during his first night on the Chicago streets:

A short-haired, dirty-white puppy, tail working, looked back over his shoulder at his master and hopped down off a curbstone. The automobile was coming fast. It didn't stop, didn't slow. The dog yelped once, sharply, and lay in the street. "Oh!" Nick gasped, scared and with pity.

The puppy lay in the gutter belching blood. His skinny legs pawed the air. A crowd, staring, pushed in on tiptoe. The puppy's head lay in an oil puddle. His blood, spewing out of his mouth, mixed with the oil. The dog's master, unconcerned, walked on down the street. (85)

The image of the dog, along with that of the mouse, is repeated, most notably and powerfully as Nick's execution draws close:

Again he was awake in pain, torture, fear, hopelessness. Awake in body and mind. Awake in his blood. Tensed. Helpless. Pinioned. Alive as are all dead things in their last strugglings for the life that is lost. Every nerve screaming. Every emotion tearing. Every blood vessel pounding.

He carried his torture into unconsciousness. The dream moved to its fortieth reel. . . . [sic]
THE MOUSE! THE MOUSE!
Live fast, die young, and have a good-looking corpse.
THE DOG!   (475)

Earlier in the novel, just as the police dragnet was closing in, Nick observed a spider stretching its web across the ceiling of the room in which he was hiding; in a sense, the image is completed on the night of his execution when Nick watches a fly caught in a spider web in his cell — trapped by the spider as Nick himself has been trapped by society. Still unable to abide cruelty — or perhaps feeling empathy with the victim — Nick releases the fly from the web before the spider can kill it. Similarly, Nick's obvious empathy with Tommy, whose beating he recalls so often, is clearly intended to influence the reader's response to Nick's execution; for recollections of Tommy's beating heighten the emotional impact of the very moment of Nick's electrocution:

> Nick shut his eyes against the blackness of the head hood. Again he saw the circle of cloth and Tommy grabbing his ankles with the skin taut across his small behind . . . saw the hard light beating down, Fuller's arm raised with the strap, like a coiled snake, ready to strike. Ready to cut the flesh, ready to bring blood and screams and sobbing, whimpering, blubbering.
> And the priest, ". . . *may he rest in peace* . . ."
> And the hands reaching toward the buttons . . . .
> And, under the death mask . . . Nick, clenching his teeth, opened his eyes to the darkness of the mask and sobbed, seeing the lash fall, bringing blood. (503–504, elipses Motley's)

The dog, the mouse, the spider, Tommy's beating — all of these images reflect the brutality and the callousness of modern society, which toys cruelly with the criminal and has a ruthless disregard for the plight of the suffering.

While no specific images are employed, Motley uses Nick's sexual life as a correlative of his general well-being or malaise. Part of Nick's charisma is the air of a stud that he adopts toward most women. He is handsome and knows it, and he enjoys the unsolicited attention of women. Emma, however, penetrates this shell, and Nick is unable to have a successful sexual relationship with her. However, at the same time he is impotent with Emma, Nick is still attracted to the lowest of prostitutes. One reason for his difficulty is that he cannot connect his "Lily Maid," as he calls Emma, with physical sex, which has been a dirty business for him, a tool used to get money from both men and women. On another level, Nick's sexual impotence represents his inability to cope with the world Emma lives in — the unexciting world of work and middle class values. Although he tries, Nick cannot succeed in that world.

Another of Motley's conscious literary techniques is his deliberate use of violence; it so permeates the book that it never allows the reader to forget that the world Nick inhabits is a jungle. The floggings that Nick and the other boys suffer in the reform school, the unnecessary beatings that Nick and Vito inflict on the jackrolling victims, the cruelty of Riley the cop, and the detailed descriptions of tortures used by the police to wring confessions from both the guilty and the innocent — all build up to the sadistic brutality of Riley's murder. Even after Riley is seriously wounded, Nick doesn't take the opportunity to escape:

He stood over Riley. . . . Nick pointed the gun down and emptied it into Riley. The lead ripped into the blue uniform. It buried itself in the big head. He kept pulling the trigger. And Nick laughed. It was a hard laugh. Bitter. Tough. Glad. He had the gun pointed down and kept pulling the trigger. The trigger made an empty, clicking sound. Blood spewed out of Riley's mouth and his nostrils. . . . Riley's eyes were hard with hate. But the pistol-barrel eyes had shot their fire. The hate was freezing out of them. They were blank, staring, glazed. Nick . . . took the gun and threw it in Riley's face.

. . . .

Nick stood looking down at Riley. . . . He remembered the rabbit punches. He lifted his foot and kicked Riley. He remembered how Riley had kicked him when he was down on his hands and knees in the basement of the police station. He kicked Riley, hard, in the stomach. (327–28)

Nick's virtual orgy of violence and revenge is avenged in turn by a society that is also harsh and violent, as Motley emphasizes in his step by step description of the execution process.

Near the end of the novel, Motley uses ironic juxtaposition of scenes to criticize the conventional morality that sends Nick to the electric chair but allows the jurors who are killing him to go about their lives with little or no consciousness of wrongdoing. In a series of short scenes (reminiscent of Frank Norris's alternating passages on the starvation death of Mrs. Hooven while Presley dines in style in *The Octopus*), Motley moves from Nick in his death row cell to the various jurors who have condemned him. One goes home eagerly and sits down to read about preparations for the execution; another, a grandmother, prays briefly for Nick, then goes to sleep contented; a third feels guilty, now that it is too late. These scenes alternate with the preparation for the execution — the last meal, the shaving of a spot on Nick's head for the electrode, the last mile

— and with glimpses of some of Nick's old friends such as Rocky, now a hobo, and Tommy, who has become a labor organizer. The effect produced is a feeling that Nick has been selected to die almost by chance, a notion that Motley emphasizes on the final page of the novel:

> Over the jail the wind blows, sharp and cold. . . . North and south runs Halsted, twenty miles long. Twelfth Street. Boys under lampposts, shooting craps, learning. Darkness behind the school where you smarten up, you come out with a pride and go look at the good clothes in the shop windows and the swell cars whizzing past to Michigan Boulevard and start figuring out how you can get all these things. Down Maxwell Street where the prostitutes stand in the gloom-clustered doorways. Across Twelfth Street either way on Peoria are the old houses. The sad faces of the houses line the street, like old men and women sitting along the veranda of an old folks' charity home. . . .
> Nick? Knock on any door down this street. (504, italics omitted)

Perhaps more successfully than any other scene in the book, the final chapter conveys Motley's feeling of sympathy for the underdogs of society, the feeling that lies at the core of the entire novel.

V   *The Reaction to* Knock on Any Door

Critical reaction to *Knock on Any Door* was highly favorable. Although Orville Prescott, who reviewed the book for the New York *Times,* felt that the minor characters tended to fall into types rather than to come alive as subtly drawn characters, he was impressed by the reality of Nick and by the sympathy he evoked in the reader. Prescott praised Motley's achievement: "No abler recruit has joined the extreme naturalist school of fiction in a long time than Mr. Motley. The grim effectiveness of his sociological reporting is beyond question and the narrative pace of his storytelling is superior to nine out of ten naturalistic novels, which so often bog down completely in excessive repetition of the most deplorable elements in urban environment. James T. Farrell doesn't have an imitator in Willard Motley, but a rival."[26] Motley was compared to another famous author of his time by Margaret Hexter, who wrote in *Saturday Review* that " 'Knock on Any Door' naturally invites comparison with 'Native Son.' For this reader, at any rate, the comparison is all in favor of the newer work."[27]

Both the *Atlantic Monthly* and *Harper's Magazine* reviewed the book favorably. The *Atlantic* reviewer, Phoebe Lou Adams, called *Knock on Any Door* "a truly remarkable first novel" which was "just as good as the publishers claim it is." She praised Motley for producing an indictment of society without resorting to tiresome preaching, and she thought the novel reflected well on him because of "its honesty, its thoroughness, its concern for the people who appear in its pages." Summing up, she noted that "Mr. Motley has contrived to do what social novelists so often miss. He has created a complete, self-contained, absolutely convincing world."[28] The *Harper's* reviewer, Katherine Gauss Jackson, was similarly enthusiastic: "His hero is a murderer; murder is made as frightful as it is; and the punishment seems justified if one believes in capital punishment at all. But the lost beauty, the pathos, the shocking inevitability in Nicky's downfall are what make this a novel of power and stature."[29]

These opinions, of course, reflect the judgment of the literary establishment. Motley fared even better with black critics of his own period. Horace R. Cayton, co-author of the sociological study of Chicago, *Black Metropolis,* wrote several reviews of the book. In *New Republic,* Cayton stressed the sociological accuracy of the novel and its potential for educating American readers about "the psychological problems arising out of the economic and social conflicts which face America and the world."[30] Cayton also praised Motley for indicating that "it doesn't matter whether it's a Jew, a Negro, a Pole, an Italian, or a plain white Gentile American" who is driven by fear; any man of any race can be expected to lash out as Nick has done if he is subjected to the same brutal conditions. In a review for the Chicago *Tribune,* Cayton acknowledged that Motley's theme had been treated by other authors, including Theodore Dreiser, but asserted that Motley told his story "more sensitively, more beautifully, more tragically" than most other writers.[31] In a feature story on Motley, Cayton wrote, "In construction and stature, in wealth of detail, in artistry of presentation, [*Knock on Any Door*] probably exceeds anything that has come out of the Chicago school of realistic writers."[32]

Arna Bontemps, black poet and novelist, called the novel "a substantial achievement by a new writer whose work is sure to be noticed and carefully evaluated."[33] Bontemps noted several of Motley's strong points: scrupulous attention to detail, good ear for speech patterns, and the ability to create a wide range of believable characters. Like many of the other reviewers, Bontemps felt that resemblances to the works of Dreiser and Wright were basically superficial, and that Motley's novel was a unique work. Black critic Philip Butcher, who reviewed the novel for *Opportunity,* saw the book as another breakthrough for the black novelist and praised Motley's sympathy for the downtrodden as well as his stylistic precision.[34]

By the summer of 1949, two years after the novel's publication, Motley rated discussion in an article entitled "America's Top Negro Authors," a distinction he shared with Richard Wright, W. E. B. DuBois, Ann Petry, Langston Hughes, and Saunders Redding.[35] Also in 1949, a scant two years after publication, *Knock on Any Door* was the subject of a literary article published in *English Journal.* As the title, "Sociology and Imagery in a Great American Novel," suggests, Motley was considered by some members of the academic world to be more than simply a writer of best sellers.[36]

The book-buying public was as enthusiastic as the reviewers. Two weeks after publication, *Knock on Any Door* had sold forty-seven thousand copies; after two years, Appleton-Century reported three hundred fifty thousand copies in print, with orders continuing to come in at the rate of six hundred to one thousand per week. The novel was sufficiently newsworthy so that *Look* ran an extensive picture feature story — "Who Made This Boy a Murderer?" — using sections from the novel in combination with photographs of actual people from the Maxwell Street–West Madison Street neighborhood. Delighted with the idea, Motley led the photographers through the bars and alleys of the area and called on friends to demonstrate the art of jackrolling for the cameras. The novel was condensed in *Omnibook Magazine* in October 1947, where it was featured on the cover. King Features Syndicate ran a newspaper comic strip feature based on the novel from December 15, 1947, to January 20, 1948, telling Nick's story in three panels per installment with brief excerpts from the novel printed below. The final commercial accolade that the country could bestow was the 1949 Columbia Pictures movie version of *Knock on Any Door,* featuring Humphrey Bogart as Nick's attorney and introducing John Derek as Nick Romano.

Finally a success after his years of obscurity, Motley was pleased at first, but soon found that it was impossible for him to do anything but play the literary lion. Before his first novel had been set in type, Motley had been invited to speak at a Midwest Writers' Con-

ference at Northwestern University. Then came the satisfying but
time-consuming tour with the *Look* staff, not to mention several
radio interviews on local stations, autograph parties at downtown
Chicago bookstores, and more purely social invitations than he
cared to respond to. Early in 1948 he fled to Battle Ground, Wash-
ington, where he rented a small ranch house and went back to work
on his second novel.

Perhaps he had a guilty conscience: assuming that *Knock on Any
Door* was safely under contract and would need no more work, he
had applied for a Newberry Library Fellowship to work on "Of
Night, Perchance of Death," a second novel that he had been writing whenever time permitted since the summer of 1943. But since
the revision of *Knock on Any Door* had taken up nearly all of his
fellowship year, the new novel was still far from finished. An angry
letter from Stanley Pargellis, head librarian at the Newberry,
arrived within two weeks of the publication of *Knock on Any
Door*. Pargellis, who had apparently read a feature article about the
lengthy rewriting process, accused Motley of bad faith in accepting
money for a project to which he was able to give so little time.[37] The
bad feeling between the Newberry committee and himself must
have marred Motley's happiness over the success of his first novel.
He later acknowledged his obligation to the Newberry by expressing his gratitude for the fellowship (and for one provided by the
Rosenwald Fund) in *We Fished All Night*.

VI   *The Lasting Importance of the Novel*

Is *Knock on Any Door* a minor masterpiece of American literature or is it simply one of the last survivors of a dying art form —
the Naturalistic novel? Although one must make allowances for a
relative lack of historical perspective, critics who read the book
soon after its publication were, for the most part, overwhelmingly
positive in their reactions. Thomas Jarrett, for example, began his
1949 article with the assertion that if the book is not necessarily *the*
great American novel, "few can say that it is not *a* great American
novel. . . ."[38]

However, after the initial excitement had passed, critics were far
from unanimous in their praise of the novel; some felt that the
novel was overly derivative and contained little that was new to
Naturalism. Clearly the book belongs to the tradition of American
urban literature that includes works such as Stephen Crane's *Mag-*

gie: A Girl of the Streets (1893), Frank Norris' *McTeague* (1899), Theodore Dreiser's *An American Tragedy* (1925), James T. Farrell's *Studs Lonigan: A Trilogy* (1935), Richard Wright's *Native Son* (1940), Ann Petry's *The Street* (1946), and Nelson Algren's *Never Come Morning* (1942) and *The Man with The Golden Arm* (1949). Had *Knock on Any Door* appeared at an early point in this Naturalistic canon, there would be little doubt as to its significance. Even some early reviewers made the obvious comparisons between Motley's novel and Dreiser's *An American Tragedy,* although most recognized that the two books are different enough to make Motley's well worth reading for its own merits. Robert A. Bone compared it with another urban tragedy when he charged that Motley's novel "leans so heavily on *Native Son* as to border to plagiarism,"[39] but this hyperbolic statement does not survive the test of a point by point examination of the two novels.

However, some critics of the 1950s continued to find lasting values in the book. Writing particularly of Chicago novelists, but also of American Naturalists in general, Alson Smith stated, "A lot of good writing has come out of this tradition [Naturalism], and Motley's rates with the best of it."[40] Walter Rideout listed the book as one of the ten radical novels of the 1940s that he considered to have "permanent literary value."[41] Finally, Blanche Gelfant considered *Knock on Any Door* a significant urban novel even though she was dissatisfied with some aspects of the book's art.[42]

The time has come for Motley's first novel to be recognized and appreciated as a minor classic of its genre. Obviously, the reviewers who went so far as to claim that Motley was the superior of Dreiser and Wright allowed a temporary enthusiasm for a new writer to obscure their perspective. It is conceivable that Motley, like other authors before him, was hurt more than he was helped by such extravagant claims for his novel. Nevertheless, the book does have sufficient social significance as an environmentalist argument and sufficient artistic merit — especially in its carefully designed portraiture of Nick Romano — to assure Motley a permanent place in American literary history.

CHAPTER 3

We Fished All Night

A MONG the burdens of the fame that came with the publication of *Knock on Any Door* was a series of requests to review books connected with black American culture. One such request came jointly from Mrs. Alfred A. Knopf, who was introduced to Motley by Carl Van Vechten, and from the Chicago *Sun;* both asked him to review Chester Himes' latest novel. Himes had begun publishing fiction while serving a sentence in an Ohio penitentiary. After his release he had published an impressive first novel, *If He Hollers Let Him Go* (1945), an angry work that evoked comparisons with Richard Wright. Anyone familiar with Motley's philosophy about racial, as opposed to social, protest would have realized that there were major areas of disagreement between the two men and would not have asked either one to review the other. However, Motley agreed to review Himes' second novel, *Lonely Crusade* (1947), although he had not yet read it.

I *The Himes Controversy*

Reading the novel, Motley found that he violently objected to its basic premise. He reported to Mrs. Knopf that he felt compelled to treat the book harshly in his review and that, while he hoped in the future to read a book by Himes that he could praise, he could only say what he truly felt about *Lonely Crusade*. The position Himes took on the separation of the races was a position that Motley had fought all his life.

Lonely Crusade is the story of Lee Gordon, a black man who goes to work for a predominantly white union that uses him as a tool to win "colored" workers for their ranks. He is approached by members of the Communist party and by the factory owner; these two factions attempt to seduce him to the left and to the right. Lee feels little sympathy with union, management, or Communists because all are white folks' organizations and the black man stands outside, alone. In addition to Lee's political dilemma, he is torn between his black wife and his white mistress.

In Motley's opinion, Himes' main theses were that all whites hate all blacks, that all black people are paranoid and hate all white people, that fear is the basis for all other emotions that black people have, and that race is the most important factor in the daily lives of Americans. Motley condemns Lee Gordon, whom Himes presented as a victim of the white world, for being a racist himself and suggests that the secondary characters are little more than caricatures of Communists, pseudo-liberal Jews, and capitalists.

Sarcastically, Motley lists the things a reader can learn from *Lonely Crusade:*

> We learn that unions will let innocent people suffer rather than lose the support of the Communist party; that unions will let an innocent man be executed if he can't swing an election for them.... But, one supposes, labor is not well thought of these days.
>
> We learn that Negroes shudder at the sight of every passing white person. But one supposes, inter-racial and race relation groups are ineffective and no understanding and co-operation has come through such groups.[1]

Motley closes the review with a statement of his own credo: "It is indeed a 'lonely crusade' for any man of any race or nationality if his life is to pivot on race or nationality and if through bitterness or pride he turns his back on the people as a whole."[2]

When Motley finished the review, he was worried about how Himes, whom he had met briefly, would react to it. Thus, on September 3, 1947, he wrote a letter to Himes to explain that he had been asked by the publisher and the *Sun* to review the novel; that, after reading it, he had almost begged off rather than write an unfavorable review; but that, upon consideration, he had felt that his integrity was at stake and had written that he truly thought. In a gracious reply, Himes, who had not yet seen the review, praised Motley for his honesty and frankness and assured him that the review would make no difference in their relationship; he closed his letter by warmly praising *Knock on Any Door.*

However, when Himes read the review, he apparently felt differently. On October 23 he wrote an angry letter to Emmett Dedmon, the book editor of the *Sun,* in which he characterized the review as vicious and malicious. Stating that Motley had deliberately distorted the point of the book, Himes quoted from *Lonely Crusade* to prove that it was not a racist novel.[3] In spite of Motley's efforts to soften the blow, he never seems to have been close to Himes after the review, and when Himes recalled the episode nearly twenty-five years later, he characterized the review as "a vicious personal attack charging me personally with statements taken from the dialogues of my characters."[4]

Aside from this disagreement with Himes, Motley seems to have been respected by other black authors of his era. Fellow Chicagoans Gwendolyn Brooks and Alden Bland sought him out, and he carried on a correspondence with Arna Bontemps, who had been an important literary figure since the Harlem Renaissance. Carl Van Vechten, a white man who had helped a number of black authors, wrote asking that Motley donate the manuscript of *Knock on Any Door* to the James Weldon Johnson Memorial Collection at Yale University, a singular honor. However, for Willard Motley, now nearing the age of forty, the important thing was to show the world that he was not a one book novelist. Most of his energy was reserved for the novel he had begun in 1943.

II   *"Of Night, Perchance of Death"*

The book that was to become *We Fished All Night* grew from two concepts that Motley had formulated in the early 1940s. As early as December 1941, he had noted in his journal that he was determined to observe people's reactions during the war for a novel that he was planning to write after *Knock on Any Door*. The basic problem as he first envisioned it was the hate generated by a war — hatred which eventually pervaded all areas of a society, rather than remaining focused on the nation's military enemies.[5] This novel he began on the night of June 1, 1943, immediately upon completing his first book; and, in spite of his publishers' demands for rewrites of *Knock on Any Door,* he had continued his work on the second novel during the tenure of his Newberry Library Fellowship. By December 1945, when he applied for a grant from the Rosenwald Fund, Motley was able to report that the first draft was about half finished. Optimistically, Motley wrote that he hoped to finish this second novel, entitled "Of Night, Perchance of Death," by September 1946 and then to begin a sequel that would carry some of the same characters into the postwar period.[6]

Except for its theme of war and its use of night as a major metaphor, the novel Motley described in his application to the Rosenwald Fund bore little resemblance to the novel that was finally published in 1951. "Of Night, Perchance of Death" was to have been somewhat shorter than it finally became — between one hundred fifty thousand and two hundred thousand words compared with the two hundred forty thousand words of *We Fished All Night* — and it was to deal only with the coming of World War II and with its characters' lives before the war. Motley intended to break with the single character emphasis he had employed in *Knock on Any Door* by using five major characters and by probing the life of each extensively. Nor did he plan to repeat the chronological development of his first book; "Of Night" would open, in the first of its three sections, with a view of each of the five characters when the war begins to affect him. The bulk of the book would be the middle section, which would focus on the boyhood of each of the five young men and on their shaping by parents, neighborhoods, schools — their total environments. Sociological as the book sounds in broad outline, Motley intended to emphasize the internal, or psychological, aspects of his characters as well as their milieu. The third section, returning to the time of crisis, was to show how each individual solved the problems engendered by the war. Although Motley does not say so, his outline suggests that the novel would end on a hopeful note rather than in the gloom that pervaded the conclusion of *Knock on Any Door*. As it was finally published, only the first 117 pages of *We Fished All Night* concerned the beginning of the war.

The planned sequel to this second novel would probably have resembled *We Fished All Night* more closely, since it was to treat the healing process following the war — the rehabilitation of the ex-soldiers and the adjustments that had to be made by an entire society. Like Don Lockwood, Aaron Levin, and Jim Norris in *We Fished All Night,* three of the five characters would return from the war as cripples — one physically injured, one mentally ill, and one sexually disturbed.

Had it been written as outlined, "Of Night, Perchance of Death" would have been more autobiographical than any of Motley's published novels. One of the characters, Dave Wilson, who has only a minor role in *We Fished All Night,* is a black youth who has grown up in a white neighborhood like the one in which Motley was reared. An unpublished short story, "One of the Family," develops the relationship between Dave and the prejudiced family of a white classmate; like a real family Motley had known as a boy, the Halls accept Dave readily but maintain strong prejudices against blacks in general, as well as Jews, Germans, and other ethnic groups. Like the young Motley, Dave feels stifled by the prejudice and bigotry of this middle class neighborhood and knows that he must leave it if he is to grow.[7] A white character, Milo, is also like Motley in his rebellion against his family's middle class world and in his determination to transcend that world by becoming a creative writer. Like Dave, Milo appears as a minor character in *We Fished All Night*.

Recognizing his lack of knowledge about war itself, Motley, who was a conscientious objector, had decided to omit the battle scenes. Probably one reason underlying his decision to present the coming of the war and the aftermath in two separate books was that he thereby avoided the necessity of treating war as it is experienced by a soldier. However, perhaps influenced by the possibility of a commercial boom in war novels, Appleton pressured Motley to combine the two projected novels into a single longer book that would cover the era between the onset of World War II and the beginnings of the Cold War with Russia. Although Motley salvaged much of his original material, many of the most subtle points of the prewar novel were lost in the union of the two books.

This increased breadth of the novel caused Motley to sacrifice closely focused treatment of specific themes. The problems of ethnic minorities are presented convincingly enough through the lives of Don Lockwood and Aaron Levin, but the more general theme of the narrowness of middle class life in America is overwhelmed by the inescapable drama of the impending war. Biographical information about Jim Norris, who is from a more typically American background than the other two, is condensed into a few scattered recollections that are never fully developed. Pressure to change his concept of the story is probably also responsible, at least in part, for Motley's loss of control in the book, a fault noted by most reviewers.

III   *Three Petty Tragedies*

We Fished All Night finally evolved into a tripartite story of three young men who participate in World War II and are affected by it in different ways. Don Lockwood, Aaron Levin, and Jim Norris all

seem normal enough before their military experience; the war, however, intensifies the existing weaknesses of the first two men and
triggers a serious psychological problem in the hitherto admirable
Norris. In the end, all three lead wasted lives. The three plots are
somewhat loosely interwoven: the three men know each other
slightly, have friends in common, and are somehow connected with
the Haines Company, a giant mail-order house near the Chicago
Loop.

Don Lockwood, who has changed his name from the "foreign
sounding" Chet Kosinski, is a third generation Polish American
from a large, poor family. Never having known his father, Don has
been reared by his rather sluttish mother and by his Old World
grandfather. In his late teens, Don begins to spend as much time as
possible away from home, especially after he is taken up by a
woman active in little theater. She encourages Don's modest talent
for acting until he is drafted and sent to North Africa, where he
loses a leg. Feeling that the great acting career he had envisioned is
lost forever, Don returns to Chicago and gets a monotonous job at
the Haines Company.

One night in Bughouse Square, Don makes a dramatic speech
defending a black speaker and attracts the attention of Tom
McCarren, a ward committeeman involved with the worst elements
in Chicago politics. McCarren realizes that the combination of
Don's political naiveté, his speaking ability, and his possible image
as a wounded veteran could make him a viable candidate for public
office and one who could be easily manipulated by the party
machine. Motivated by vanity and a vague desire to help people,
Don accepts McCarren's proposal to run for state representative.
McCarren directs an outrageously dishonest campaign, beginning
with fraud and progressing to violence, but Don is defeated by an
angry citizenry. McCarren then employs him as a "bag man," a
collector of bribes and kickbacks. Having learned how an efficient
machine politician operates — and having developed a taste for
power and money — Don is eventually able to depose McCarren
and to become the ward committeeman himself. He marries Irene
Matthews, the beautiful daughter of a Chicago millionaire, and
would seem to have achieved the American Dream, albeit a somewhat tarnished version.

However, the end of the novel finds him disillusioned and dissatisfied. His wife is unfaithful, and his material possessions seem
inadequate compensation for his strictly limited role as just one

more cog in the party machine. Crowds are a sort of narcotic for him, and he is happy only when he is talking into a microphone, holding the people in his spell. His artificial leg removed to remind throngs of listeners of his wound, Don has become an actor after all.

Also ambitious when he is introduced, Aaron Levin, an uncommonly bright high school student, wants to be a poet. Like Lockwood, Aaron comes from an immigrant home in which there is only one parent. Aaron's father, a Jew who emigrated from Russia as a boy, was deserted years ago by his wife. A neighbor, Rebecca Friedman, loves Aaron, but he is oblivious of her. An outsider at school, he seeks friends among the writers and *poseurs* who frequent Bughouse Square near the Newberry Library. After his graduation, Aaron is drafted in spite of his crippling neurotic fears for his physical safety, for he gets only a moment of the psychiatrist's time during his medical examination.

Aaron, who comes home from the war in disgrace, spends most of his time crying in his room; he can't sleep or eat, his hands shake, and he wets the bed. Gradually the reader finds out that in Europe Aaron had deserted his platoon, which was entirely wiped out by a German attack. Aaron was courtmartialed, and his insanity was treated as simple cowardice until he poisoned himself while working in a military hospital. After treatment, he was released as psychologically unfit for service. Because he now feels that Rebecca is too good for him, he will have nothing to do with her; but she continues to try to help him regain his sanity until he rejects her sexually. Then she becomes Lockwood's mistress.

Aaron tries to rebuild his life by finding a faith to live by. He seeks salvation in Communism; but, disillusioned, he voluntarily commits himself to a government hospital where he undergoes shock treatments and counseling and is once more released as cured. Back in Chicago, both Catholicism and Judaism fail to fulfill his needs. His only remaining faith is in himself, as a writer; however, he never finishes any work. In his final state, Aaron has lost touch with reality. Rebecca, rejected by Lockwood, moves in with Aaron to try to save him; but, instead, he pulls her down to his level. Pregnant with his child, she drinks, loses her job at the Haines Company, and becomes as much a derelict as Aaron, who is last seen sitting on a curb, writing his latest "poem," his pockets bulging with earlier poems and notes that he has forgotten.

The third subject of the novel, Jim Norris, is a charismatic, handsome young man. Jim, a former Haines employee, goes to work as a union organizer. Unlike Don, he is selfless, hoping only to raise the standard of living among workers. Jim's commitment to the union is exceeded only by his love for his wife Louise and for his small child. Since high school, Jim has been an all-American boy, popular, athletic, yet intellectually sharp and active. Before the war, he is almost too flawless to be believed. Of the three protagonists, only Jim enlists in the army to do his part to help win the war. Jim returns from the army apparently unscathed, though restless and a bit shaken by some of his experiences. The first symptom of his psychological malaise is his inability to make love to Louise, but it later becomes clear that his wife, his family, and his union job are dull and uninteresting to him now.

Gradually Jim's war experiences are revealed. He saw too many dead men and killed too many people himself. In particular, two of his own crimes disturb him: he shot a woman who was attempting to save her guerilla son, and he made love to a French prostitute who, he later discovered, was only fourteen years old. Because this incident has become Jim's obsession, he is at once horrified by and perversely attracted to young girls. For some time he just watches girls and fights his impulses by sleeping with a wide variety of women and by drinking more than in the past. He is fascinated by news accounts of child molestation and rape, and on one occasion finally follows a girl into a park, grabs her, and then lets her go without harming her. After blacking out during a drinking bout, he awakens in jail and discovers that he is charged with raping an eleven year old girl. Though he is released because the girl can't identify him, Jim fears that he actually had committed the crime; but he continues to follow other girls at night. Jim is saved from himself when he is killed by a police club during a strike against the Haines Company. He dies a martyr for the union in which he no longer believes.

Motley's last scenes emphasize the bitterness of his view of the postwar world. Organized labor, whose future seemed hopeful for a time, now seems to be losing its fight. Anti-Semitism and racial hatred, dormant during the war, are now on the rise. Although the lives of a whole generation of young men have been ruined, preparations are being made for another war. Don Lockwood, the least sympathetic of the three protagonists, is the only one left in possession of his faculties; and he has survived only by becoming thoroughly corrupt.

IV   *Second Novel Trouble*

Critical reaction to Motley's second novel was much less favorable than it had been to *Knock on Any Door.* Reviewing *We Fished All Night* for the New York *Times,* Orville Prescott, who had been impressed with Motley's first book, reported that "Mr. Motley's second novel ... isn't even minor league material compared with its predecessor. As a work of fiction, it's strictly amateur." Prescott noted that Motley had worked hard on the novel for five years but that its defects tended to outweigh its merits:

With an intense emotion which often lured him into painfully rapturous excesses of style, with furious determination to express his deepest convictions about society and his intimate knowledge of the seamy side of Chicago, Mr. Motley poured out a torrent of words, more than 240,000 of them. They include some good things — grimy passages of relentless realism, sharply accurate glimpses of the thought and speech and customs of various minority groups. But for every page of effective writing ... there are a dozen exasperatingly bad ones.[8]

More specifically, Prescott charged that the book was not a finished novel but "the raw material for a novel," that the book had not been adequately revised. Its ideas seemed to him undigested — not so much fully enunciated concepts as "two powerful emotions.... Both are admirable. The first is a feeling of human brotherhood, of the common humanity of everyone no matter what his race, his religion, his accent or his color. The second is rage against war, the infinite suffering caused by the last one and the general dread of the next. But Mr. Motley has failed to use these emotions successfully in fictional terms." On the whole, Prescott displayed good will toward Motley, for he attributed the failure of the novel to the traditional "second novel trouble" that has bothered many novelists who have had one major success.

Many reviewers were much less kind and balanced in their treatment of the book. To Frank Getlein of *Commonweal,* it seemed a "worthless novel," which oversimplified the conflict between capital and labor and which fell back on the old cliché of the city as "painted woman" that corrupts young men who start out with high ideals. Getlein also complained: "Never content with saying a thing once if he can possibly say it seven times, Mr. Motley dittoes his scenes of city-hall and board-room corruption until, toward the end of the run, he is burlesquing himself on every page."[9] The reviewer for *Time* took a similar tack: "If sincerity were enough to make a good novel, *We Fished All Night* might be a minor masterpiece. It has a few vivid moments: a comic meeting of ward heelers, a warm glimpse of a Polish family. But for the most part its political sermonizing stirs unhappy memories of the 'proletarian fiction' of the 1930s. In 560 closely printed pages, that is too much of a bad thing."[10]

In *Nation,* Harvey Swados dismissed the story of Don Lockwood as a cliché and criticized the novel's philosophical framework: "At times he seems to be saying that the war warped American young men, but we know now that ... our ex-soldiers ... have not become either nihilists or killers, not even those who have lost limbs. At other times he seems to be writing a proletarian novel, imputing the misery of his heroes to their miserable and poverty-stricken boyhoods and to the greed of a senile factory owner; but the main direction of American life has long since turned away from that indicated by the novelists of this school."[11]

Expressing his respect for the novel's "earnestness and conscientiousness," James Gray, writing for *Saturday Review,* pronounces it a failure because of "its inability to reach the mind or the heart." After comparing *We Fished All Night* unfavorably to *Knock on Any Door,* he criticizes Motley's approach to Naturalism: "Passion seems to have been replaced by a kind of dogged thoroughness which serves only to blunt the author's purpose. 'We Fished All Night' should have been a latter-day 'Germinal.' But Zola, despite all his own limitations, was much more the master of the scene, much more the intuitive student of the human heart than his disciple has yet learned to be."[12]

Thus, most reviewers for national journals emphasized the novel's failures and only grudgingly noted its positive qualities, as in Harvey Swados' remark that the novel had a "superficial correspondence to the facts of American life — so that to Europeans they probably have the quality of revelations...."[13] However, the reviews closer to home were more friendly. Chicago, with its complex about being America's "second city," has always tended to elevate its authors in a spirit of provincial patriotism. Robert Cromie introduced the book to Chicago *Tribune* readers by reminding them of Motley's earlier success and assuring them that his "second novel should do nothing to dim the brightness."[14] Van Allen Bradley, of the Chicago *Daily News,* was more cautious, beginning with the observation that the novel was "remarkable for its curious admixture of strength and weaknesses." However, he went on to say, "It is written with fire and rage and compassion. It has powerful moments of passion and occasional peaks of beauty. It has ugliness and squalor, brutality and obscenity. In some respects it is a better novel than 'Knock on Any Door.' In others it falls short of that impressive performance."[15]

While Motley may have been comforted by these bits of home town puffery, he had to face the fact that his second novel was considered a disappointment after his powerful first work. He had attempted to grow as an author — to move away from the single intense story of one character's life and death to variations on a theme through the stories of several major characters. Instead of cashing in on his reputation as a writer who specialized in crime and juvenile delinquency, he had attempted to write a panoramic novel that would examine an entire society. But few reviewers acknowledged his attempts to broaden his subject matter and to use different techniques, nor did they concede that he might learn even through his errors. None commented on his efforts to modify the relatively simple style that he had employed in *Knock on Any Door*; instead they implied that Motley would have done better to serve more of the same fare that he had given his readers in his first novel. The critical reaction was especially disappointing in view of the ambitions he had entertained for his second novel.

V   *An Impressive Failure*

There were several valid reasons for the adverse reactions to Motley's second novel. In *Knock on Any Door* he had planned from the beginning to write a book with a critical view of the inequities and abuses of power in law enforcement agencies and penal institutions. Whatever the origins of his difficulty with his second book, no such single thesis runs clearly through it. Rather, as some of the reviewers wrote, Motley either has too many targets or is confused about where to place the blame for the sickness of a whole society in the twentieth century.

One of the theses is that war is an evil influence on mankind, that it warps a whole society — from the active participants, who may suffer its after effects for the rest of their lives, to the people on the "home front," who retain the hatred and prejudice bred by the war long after it is over. Motley's original conception of the postwar book, with its three protagonists crippled physically, mentally, and morally, might have been more direct in its condemnation of war than *We Fished All Night.* A reader might qeustion whether World War II was in fact responsible for the tragedies that befall the principal characters.

Something of an opportunist before the war, Don Lockwood uses Sue Carroll; he makes love to her so that she will help him with his acting and give him better roles in her productions. Meanwhile, his roving eye notes younger and prettier girls, and he tries to use his small theatrical successes to interest them. His attitude toward his family is no less self-centered; for, although treated indulgently by his family, he keeps its very existence a secret. He rejects even his kindly grandfather, feeling that it is a mark of shame to be identified with a Polish immigrant. Don accepts the sacrifices the family makes (such as giving him a room of his own in a two room apartment while the other five members of the family eat and sleep in the remaining room) as if they are his just due; after all, he is handsomer and smarter than the rest. While the reader may understand that Don is a product of the poverty of his early life, he lacks the charm of a Nick Romano and is rarely considered sympathetically.

By crippling Don, the war magnifies some of his least admirable traits: he becomes even more self-centered and more subject to fits of self-pity. At the same time, the fact that he is wounded makes other people less critical of him and more inclined to overlook his faults. Tom McCarren, the political boss, sees Don pretty much as he is — handsome, selfish, and visibly wounded — and merely capitalizes on Don's character traits during the campaign. The reader may well doubt that Don would have been any better a person if he had not gone to war. Ironically, the war also has had a slight positive influence on Don in that he has met an idealistic young man, Wayne, who was killed in the same battle in which Don lost his leg. Everything Don was not, Wayne was the product of a stable family and neighborhood; he looked forward to college, to marriage with a childhood sweetheart, and to a life of service to others after the war. All of Don's fleeting decent impulses in his postwar life stem from his thoughts of Wayne and of how Wayne might have acted.

Before the war, Aaron Levin is a sympathetic character, although he obviously has some psychological problems. He feels shame for his Jewish heritage and the Old World ways of his father, much as Don feels about his heritage and his family. Sexually maladjusted, probably because of his dim memories of his mother, he rejects his neighbor Rebecca, who loves him. Aaron's ambition to be a writer seems to have its roots in a desire to be more important, just as Don seeks a better image by playing parts on the stage. Aaron's tragedy is perhaps not so much that the war has caused him to lose his mind, but that it has aggravated a condition that might have emerged even in civilian life.

Of the three principals, Jim Norris is the only one who seems well adjusted before the war. He is happy in his marriage and in his work as a union organizer. However, it is not only the war that unbalances Jim's moral sense, but the fact that he is far from home and is no longer inhibited by the expectations of those who know him. A cynic might rightly suggest that a convention trip to Atlantic City would have had much the same effect on Jim. Nevertheless, some of the traumata Jim suffers belong distinctly to the war — for example, his nauseating experiences as a member of the Grave Registration Detail, or the occasions when he has killed fleeing men or watched others shoot down helpless prisoners. On the other hand, his fascination with young girls and his fear that he will molest a child do not stem from his encounter with the young French prostitute but from a long-repressed childhood experience which Jim finally remembers:

> It was almost as if he were looking down into a toy street, into a nightmare. The street lamps leaned awry. The crooked, warped floor to the hall toilet in the slum house, West Side, Chicago. The boy was himself. The girl was his sister. They were eight and nine years old. Their mother had caught them in their innocent explorations of each other's bodies. Their mother's hard hand across their faces and heads. His sister had screamed and dropped her skirt down. In fear he had urinated down the front of his pants. It was bad, bad, bad! For a week it was bad. For a month. Forever. He had never gotten over his mother's face and eyes and mouth saying it was bad, bad, bad![16]

As with Don and Aaron, Jim's wartime experiences aggravated a condition that antedates the war. However, in Jim's case more than in the others, Motley leaves the impression that a successful adjustment has been undone. Jim's marriage and the sublimation he achieves by throwing himself into his job so vigorously might have proved to be an effective therapy had it not been for World War II.

Distracting the reader's attention from the antiwar theme of the novel is a second powerful strand that is not successfully woven with the first; this secondary emphasis is Motley's condemnation of crooked machine politics. By going into great detail about Don's involvement with Chicago politics, Motley diluted the importance of the three parallel lives that had originally given structure to the novel; thus, some critics (and the writer who did the copy for the Appleton dust jacket) identified the novel as primarily Don's story. Unlike the antiwar theme, which seems vague and tenuous, the political theme of the novel is well-documented but perhaps oversimplified. All of the machine politicians exhibit a dog-eat-dog immorality that enables them to turn on any of their fellows who display signs of weakness; this trait eventually allows Don to supplant McCarren by showing his precinct captains that McCarren is losing his authority. Acting in their own self-interest, the politicians support Don as wholeheartedly as they had ever supported McCarren.

There is merit in the way in which Motley attacks big city politics. Relentlessly he exposes the specific tricks used by the Chicago Democratic machine: rival candidates are bribed or blackmailed into removing themselves from the slate; vagrants are bribed for their votes; criminals are released from jail for a promise to deliver their votes; crooked police on poll duty spy on voters; poll watchers are forced from their posts by threats; the chain vote assures precinct captains that promises are being kept; whole ballot boxes are destroyed by deliberately set fires in precincts where the vote is not favorable to the machine. Graft is treated with similar thoroughness as Motley shows how laws are not enforced against operators of shady businesses and members of organized crime if they know the right people and pay the right price. Bookies, policy kings, and owners of bars known for questionable practices all work closely with political figures. Emerson Bradley, the businessman, secures the services of the city police as strikebreakers in return for the promise of "campaign funds" that go into the pockets of McCarren and his cronies; Bradley also obtains city land for a low price by paying the requisite bribes.

On the other hand, Motley is less successful in his use of Don as the primary exponent of this theme. Superficially, the antiwar theme and the political theme are related by Don's experience. As a crippled veteran, he makes a good candidate; billing him as the first man wounded in World War II, McCarren runs him unsuccessfully for state representative. Don, still hoping to do something decent in memory of the dead Wayne, displays incredible naiveté as he plays along with McCarren's scheme:

Don walked proudly in the night. Jesus Christ, it was something to brag
about! Running for office! Having a big man, a powerful man like Mr.
McCarren backing him. And yes ... he could live Wayne's life for him.
He could do the things Wayne would have done.... the Democrats ...
the merits of their cause were good. The principles of F. D. R. Those principles that Truman would follow. Sue would be proud of him.... Wayne
hadn't died in vain....
     These, the days of his triumph ....   (330)

While his egotism is well-realized, as in the above passage, it is
difficult to understand why Don feels that his elevation will serve
noble purposes or how such an innocent dupe could so quickly
become boss of North Side politics. The reader simply does not see
enough of the step-by-step disintegration of Don's character to be
able to accept his transition from a basically weak egotist who pas-
sively follows orders to a ruthless plotter who is capable of taking
over a major segment of the Chicago political machine.
     The political and antiwar themes struggle for dominance
throughout the Lockwood portions of the novel, but they are far
from being the only major concerns. In fact, the opening of the
novel suggests the thematic importance of the conflict between
capital and labor in three pages of powerful, sometimes almost lyrical prose and a wealth of provocative symbols. Representing capital is the alabaster building with the bronze plaque proclaiming:
"THE HAINES COMPANY: A Nation Within A Nation." The
skyscraper "is said to be the most beautiful, powerful and wonder-
ful of all. It rises in twin buildings, one on either side of the river.
One seems to mirror the other. One seems reality; the other the
dream" (2). Motley elaborates: "The huge stanchions of the building thrust up and out mightily. The concrete, the marble, was built
to last forever. Rub your hand across it. It is cold as ice. The people
are just the pulp to be used by the building" (2).
     Alternating with the suggestive references to the building are
paragraphs describing the Haines Company's president and its
workers: Emerson Bradley's "old and wrinkled face has the look of
one accustomed to command. You can see, too, in his face, all the
drinks he has drunk, all the steaks he has eaten, all the women he
has slept with" (2). And the workers, "from streetcar and El and
shuffling close together like a herd of cattle, come up the broad
marble steps, in through the wall of glass doors... delivering backs
for lifting, fingers for file cabinets and typewriters" (2). Image
piled on image conveys Motley's intense sympathy for these

exploited workers, but his specific details have extended meanings so that the reader realizes that the conflict is not limited to the Haines Company.

For example, "Emerson Bradley is a duplication of the deity.... If we all forsake him he will die of hunger. Who will pick his cotton? Who will manufacture his goods for him?" (3). Mythical overtones are added later when Jim Norris describes the building as a "colossus that spans the river" and Bradley as a "cyclops who can see but one way" (52). Jim's rousing speech to the workers also integrates the present battle with the history of man's progress in phrases reminiscent of Carl Sandburg's *The People, Yes*: Man "has traveled a long, weary road. All the sweat and blood that has been spilled at machines and in factories has not been spilled in vain.... You can't stop the people in their forward march. The people, like ants, live by co-operating. They — the Emerson Bradleys — can't divide man against man forever" (54).

Motley also augments the significance of the company-labor conflict with his descriptions of the figures who represent each side. Blond and bronzed, Norris seems the epitome of handsome youth and virility as he addresses the union rally: "His large, hair-curled arms were upraised, his angry voice rang with indignation.... He pointed his long, tanned and muscular arm...." On the platform, "the thighs of his legs showing above the tightly packed heads, he looked like an athlete. Slightly over six feet tall, his shoulders were square and broad, his hips slim in the blue faded tight-fitting trousers..." (52). On the other hand, Bradley's toadlike appearance suggests his corrupt character:

Emerson Bradley, seventy-five years old, was a small, short man, inclined toward obesity, baldheaded, with an aggressive jaw and a stubby, bristled gray mustache.... His old face was an ashy pink and through the pink-polished scalp of his bald, bulbous head muddy-blue ropes of veins showed. His nose was large and loose on his frowning face with fleshy lines coming down either side of it to a thick mouth under which his aggressive, thrust-out chin was wrinkled like a prune.... The eyelids were the loose flesh of a turkey's neck and much the same color and, half-drooped, gave his face the appearance of perpetual peevishness. (91–92)

Not only his appearance but his perverted, cruel character contributes to this personification of decadent capitalism. It seems significant that Motley tells us about Bradley, "now, an old man with heart trouble, he had page girls come to his office and entertain him in an unusual way" (99). In contrast with Bradley, who enjoys his perversion, Norris is driven to despair by his abnormal sexual desires and is absolved from blame only by his dying effort "in the name of the people, the little people who seeded the entire world, who grew like grass across the world, who withered and died or who were cut down in youth" (559).

Thus, early in the novel Motley has clearly drawn the battle lines: he has pitted beautiful hero against debauched villain, and he has established the twin skyscrapers as the dominant symbols of the conflict. Unfortunately, these promises of future significance and drama prove misleading; instead of the heroic archetypal struggle the reader has been led to expect, the Haines Company plot appears only intermittently and takes up fewer than one hundred pages in the five hundred and sixty page novel. Like Don Lockwood, Bradley is "the power," a corrupt and detestable robber baron. When the Haines Company is threatened by a strike, Bradley counters by showing workers a propaganda movie, "The Happy Worker," that depicts a faithful employee who is receiving his just rewards over the years. However, measures taken to break the strike become progressively more stern, for absent workers are fired and their places are filled by others who have been bribed with such scarce items as nylon stockings. Court orders to restrain picketing are brutally enforced by Chicago police. Bradley's treatment of his customers is similarly ruthless. When people fail to pay promptly for shoddy mail-order merchandise, a special department employs a series of dirty tricks designed to ruin the debtor's reputation and credit rating. Most people soon pay when they are threatened with legal action and are embarrassed by dunning telegrams at their places of employment.

Unfortunately, as in the case of the antiwar theme, Motley undercuts the capital-labor conflict and dissipates its forcefulness. D. S. Matthews, a rough diamond who has made a fortune as a plumbing contractor, seems invented to present a favorable view of the capitalist. We first see him drinking hard at an American Legion dance, showing that he is not too good to mingle with ordinary folk. He always dresses in a wrinkled suit and scuffed shoes, and his huge calloused hands betray his lower class origins. On the other hand, his daughter Irene, who marries Don Lockwood, is a tramp who behaves like a stereotype of a spoiled rich girl.

Motley seems to suggest that families run in cycles, that inherited wealth is a corrupting influence of which the self-made man is free.

This theory is supported by the fact that, during the strike, Bradley's granddaughter marches with the strikers, thus offering hope that the Bradley family may once more establish contact with the common people. However, if Motley's intention is to show the difference in generations, he does not make the message clear. At best, the reader may decide that Motley is being scrupulously fair by presenting two very different capitalists; at worst, a reader may suspect that the author really has no social theory, that he confuses his readers because he himself is not sure which position he wishes to adopt.[17]

Clearly, the labor theme is not presented as strongly or as persistently as it might have been, and the reader's expectations are disappointed as this theme gets lost among the antiwar and anti–political machine plot lines. However, the capital-labor plot has a formal function as well as a thematic one; it serves as introduction and conclusion to the novel, providing a sort of envelope structure. The labor dispute in which Jim is killed dominates the last pages; Motley deliberately repeats early descriptive passages at the end; and most of the people mentioned on page three in the first section are present in the wrap-up scenes in the last chapter. In effect, the capital-labor plot unifies the major plot lines, just as the night of the riot brings the three main characters together: an abstracted Aaron sits on a curb near the riot area; Jim is struck down in the riot; and the "good American" Don is on crutches addressing the workers who have not yet joined the rioters.

While the novel begins with a cheerful and patriotic description of soldiers coming back from war, it ends with a depressing view of soldiers' bodies being returned to the United States. Leading the reader to draw the parallel with the three wasted lives of the main characters, the author emphasizes the waste of war: "Man will forget. The wind blows, the dust blows, the sand blows.... The young grass is cut down. The new grass grows up. To be cut down. Night, night, night, and the wind. Why does God waste so many seeds?" (560, italics omitted). All three themes are thus united; whether the war is against a foreign enemy, a corrupt political machine, or an exploiting capitalist, the little people comprise the army and are ultimately destroyed. As Motley says both early and late in the novel, "The people are just the pulp to be used..." (2 and 557). The futility of the three lives defines the significance of the novel's title.

In addition to the three major themes, two minor themes merit

attention. One of Motley's original ideas from "Of Night, Perchance of Death," the growth of the artist in a middle class American environment, is reflected in Aaron's story. Perhaps there is an
element of self-parody in the fact that the young Aaron romanti-
cally aspires to a career as a writer, imitates the literature he has
read, and writes his poems with a quill pen, just as Motley did when
he was young. However, unlike Motley, Aaron is warped by his war
experience and never comes to grips with reality in his writing.
Insights into the literary life of Chicago are offered when the
youthful Aaron meets various literary *poseurs* as well as genuinely
talented writers, but packed into a novel that offers so many other
currents and ideas, the theme of the artist's growth is not developed
fully enough to do it justice. The most successful episodes along
this line deal with Aaron's attempts to write fiction based on his
battle experiences and to bend his art to the will of the Communist
party.

The beginning of Aaron's war novel — intended to preclude another conflict by presenting the full horror of World War II — is
powerful enough to win Milo's enthusiastic approval, but Aaron
destroys it when he sees the postwar society going mindlessly about
its business, doing nothing to prevent the growth of the Cold War
and the building of nuclear arsenals. The healing process that
began when Aaron started to write is halted, and he regresses, drift-
ing purposelessly again.

After attending a worker's school for some weeks, Aaron's
enthusiasm for the Communist party leads him to join the staff of
the school newspaper. Like Ralph Ellison's Invisible Man, Aaron is
given menial tasks such as stuffing envelopes as a token of the discipline he must accept. Finally allowed to write an article, he works
over it for three days, only to be told that it is full of naive errors.
After several revisions, Aaron thinks he has grasped the truth, but
his teacher is horrified: "How can you say that you will willingly
give up freedom of expression? How can you imply that this is what
the Party demands? Capitalistic society does not allow freedom of
expression. Freedom of expression only comes when a society completely controls itself, and capitalism does not control its own economic and social life.... I'm afraid, Aaron, you will have to work
very hard to rid yourself of the bourgeois idea that self-control
means loss of freedom..." (236). When Aaron finally writes the
article successfully, it is by paraphrasing a section of a Marxist
book. Offered membership in the party, he declines, since he finds

that he has been reduced to an automaton, writing to support the party line. While this episode is an interesting commentary on the writer's need for freedom, it is not an integral part of the overall design of the novel.

A final theme on which Motley touches briefly is racism, an attitude that has been encouraged by the war. Propaganda directed against the Japanese has frequently taken the form of racial slurs, and strong prejudice against Orientals continues into the postwar era. Moreover, Americans who came to the defense of German Jews still look down on American Jews, as Motley shows in a series of incidents when Don takes Rebecca Friedman to an American Legion dance, where other guests make snide remarks about her; once Don himself Americanizes her name when introducing her because he is embarrassed to be seen with a Jewish girl. Dave Wilson, the black character who was to have played an important part in the novel as Motley first planned it, appears in a few scenes of *We Fished All Night* and sometimes has to cope with racial prejudice.

Motley suggests that prejudice has been burned out of some men who served in the military when he introduces Ollie, a young Southerner who was in the navy with Max, a Mexican friend of Dave's from high school. Dave wonders whether Max has prepared Ollie for the fact that his old friend is black. His apprehensions evaporate when Max stands like a symbol of unity between them: ''The Mexican boy pushed in between them in his sailor's uniform and threw an arm around the shoulders of each. His light tan face shone in many highlights as it tightened with his grin and his black, black eyes hid in little slits. 'Dave,' he said to the Negro, 'this is Ollie.' 'Ollie,' he said to the southern boy, 'this is Dave.' And Max grinned again, looked proudly from one to the other'' (150). This passage epitomizes Motley's own racial attitude and hopes as he expressed them in statements and in nonfiction but rather seldom in his fiction.

The main reason for the failure of the novel, then, is Motley's attempt, partially in response to the wishes of the publisher, to introduce far too many causes. Any one of the many themes he juggled in *We Fished All Night* could have been the basis of a novel of ordinary length. What resulted from his effort to unite the two books he had planned was an uneasy alliance of diverse themes, none of which is treated adequately. What readers and reviewers witnessed was a talent that had gone out of control, a novelist who seemed to have ignored the advice of William Dean Howells, who cautions the novelist against merely heaping up facts without sufficiently interpreting their significance.[18]

On the other hand, Motley's second novel was not the unalloyed failure described by some critics, such as Robert A. Bone.[19] Motley had made a definite effort to develop his abilities, to go beyond what he had accomplished in *Knock on Any Door,* and in many ways *We Fished All Night* is far more sophisticated than his first book. One example of his greater literary sophistication is the title, based on a rough paraphrase of Peter's statement to Christ (Luke 5:5) which Motley rendered "Lord, we fished all night and caught nothing" ([xi]). One immediate irony is the fact that, unlike the biblical context, Motley's story contains no miracles. In fact, he emphasizes throughout the book that no Christ was forthcoming to turn the weariness of defeat into a dramatic victory. Those of Motley's characters who do have the faith to cast out once again after fishing all night are rewarded only with more and sometimes even deeper disappointments. Don loses the last of his meager integrity, Aaron becomes completely insane, and Jim Norris escapes degradation through death.

The six books of the novel are related to the expression "we fished all night" by their titles and prevailing themes. Book One, "Watchman, What of the Night?" which is based on a second biblical allusion to night, recalls the fall of Babylon in the Old Testament (Isaiah 21:11); Book Two, "Evening," heralds the coming darkness of war; and Book Three, "Dawn," suggests that the worst is over. True, the young men who have fished all night through the dark of the war have received nothing but physical and psychic injuries, but now they are presumably coming home to mend and to make something of their lives. Babylon has not fallen. At the end of "Dawn," however, there are still four hundred pages of defeats, disappointments, and tragedies before the rest of Motley's story is told.

The titles of the last three books, "Evening," "Evening Darkens," and "Watchman, What of the Night?" indicate another cycle of hatred, conflict, and spiritual poverty. The second night, the darkness of the postwar world, is more ominous in its own way than the darkness of war. People could live with the war, which would end someday; but the postwar darkness of bigotry, ignorance, dishonesty, want, and despair seems to be a chronic condition of man — one partially brought on by his own character. The final scenes of the book reinforce the significance of the title and the epigraph. It is literally night in the city as the reader sees the protagonists for the last time. Jim is sinking into the permanent night of death, and Aaron into the night of insanity as he scribbles down a line of poetry, unconsciously copied from James Thomson's "The City of Dreadful Night." Ironically, Aaron regards his plagiarized line, "the city was of night, perchance of death, but certainly of night," as "the best thing he had ever written" (556). Don is in the grip of the "Mr. Veteran" image that the political machine created; there is no escape back to his decent aspirations. By reusing the titles of Book One and Book Two, Motley suggests the lack of progress made by mankind, the circularity of the fruitless quest for a better world.

Besides the titles of the books, Motley uses epigraphs at the beginnings of some chapters and sections. Taken from the Book of Proverbs in the Old Testament, these epigraphs attach symbolic meanings to the three principal characters. Don becomes "an eagle in the air" (Proverbs 30:18–19) and "a serpent upon a rock" (Proverbs 30:19), both symbols of beauty and power in their biblical context but used with some degree of irony by Motley. Aaron is identified with the ants, "a people not strong" (Proverbs 30:24–25) and Jim with "the locusts [who] have no king yet go they forth all of them in bands" and with the spider who is found even within king's palaces (Proverbs 30:27–28).

Although the proverbs correlate with only some aspects of the three characters — Don's physical appearance, Aaron's weakness, and Jim's involvement with the masses — the biblical quotations add to the solemn tone of the novel and relate the current tragedies to man's age-old wisdom, much as do the title and the heading of the first and last chapters. One epigraph, "lost, and by the wind grieved," which occurs just five pages from the end, captures the tone and significance of the conclusion of the novel. Unlike the others, this quotation is from Thomas Wolfe's novel *Look Homeward, Angel,* specifically from the narrator's poetic elegy on his dead brother Ben, a passage that emphasizes the same feelings Motley evokes at the end of *We Fished All Night*: tragedy, hopelessness, loss, and a sense of the cyclical nature of life.[20]

Besides Motley's skillful development of the title motif, he achieved other small artistic successes in the novel. His use of actual headlines and excerpts from popular songs of the era, a technique learned from John Dos Passos, effectively recreates the aura of postwar America. As Aaron struggles to regain his own sanity, the world around him seems to be willfully losing its collective sanity, as documented by such headlines as:

> Defense Against
> A-Bomb Possible (260)
>
> Russia Has A-Bomb
> U.S. has Stock Pile of A-Bombs (261)
>
> Hershey Tells
> Nation's Need
> For Killers (264)

Similarly, while Jim Norris drinks in "Nick's Veteran Bar," one line from the song "Route 66" occurs over and over. As various veterans compete with each other telling sadistic war stories, the jukebox comments like a chorus: "You get your kicks." The point is clear: these men have learned to "get their kicks" from the seduction and gang rapes of European women and the ruthless slaying of disarmed enemy soldiers. Their desires to relive the events when the war is over show the extent of their degeneracy. This picture of American fighting men who have been brutalized by their experience was criticized by some reviewers in a political rather than an artistic reaction to the novel, but some of Motley's most telling thrusts at the war are achieved in the barroom scenes.

With the creation of the three main characters of *We Fished All Night,* Motley had deliberately departed from his practice in *Knock on Any Door,* in which he had told a composite story of two boys he knew and liked and emphasized the sympathetic characteristics of his protagonist. Of the three men in the second novel, only Jim Norris evokes much sympathy from the reader; indeed, some reviewers were critical of these antiheroes, as if only sympathetic characters were worth reading about. By focusing on relatively unattractive characters, Motley sought to achieve a more objective stance and to break away from the role of a writer captivated by his own creation. By employing three central characters plus a host of secondary figures, he attempted to transcend one limitation of *Knock on Any Door,* in which Nick so thoroughly overshadows all others that the minor characters seem poorly realized.

Among the critics of the early 1950s, only Nick Aaron Ford chose to emphasize the skill that Motley evidenced in weaving the stories of his three protagonists throughout the fiber of American society.[21] By making Don a Pole and Aaron a Jew, Motley could explore two distinct ethnic groups of his native Chicago, as he had done with the Italians in his first book. The research behind these two characterizations is sound; Don and his grandfather and Aaron and his father are vivid pairs who effectively exemplify some of the problems faced by first generation immigrants and by their Americanized descendants. The portraiture found in this novel is reminiscent of the works of James T. Farrell.

Another aspect of the characterization in *We Fished All Night* that critics might have appreciated more is Motley's increased awareness of the importance of secondary characters. Even some critics who liked *Knock on Any Door* commented on the rather shallow nature of its minor characters. In *We Fished All Night* Motley creates a number of successful secondary figures. Milo and Steve are convincing as a dedicated writer and a precious literary bore, respectively. O'Keefe, the elevator operator at the Haines Company, is a vividly drawn old union man. Sue Carroll, the aging little theater director, is well realized, as is Louise Norris, Jim's wife. Except for a few overdrawn politicians, Motley is invariably deft in his creation of a whole world of supporting characters who provide the rich background of the novel and contribute so much to its verisimilitude.

Another clear indication of Motley's technical advancement is his far more imaginative use of time in *We Fished All Night* than in his first novel, which was predominantly chronological. By employing the flashback skillfully, he introduces elements of suspense, letting the reader know part of a character's war experience at one time and saving other revelations for later in the novel. This technique is especially effective in Motley's treatment of Aaron, whose perceptions and memories are distorted by his mental illness, but delayed knowledge of Wayne and the occasion of Don's wounding also adds to the impact of Don's story. The flashback technique is particularly appropriate to the psychological level of Jim's story because it reinforces the idea that Jim, consciously or unconsciously, has repressed certain memories; as in psychoanalysis, it is only gradually that these memories surface and trace his sexual abnormality back to its ultimate origin.

Thus, while *We Fished All Night* cannot be counted as a commercial or a literary success, it represents a significant stage in the development of the author. It was necessary at this point in Motley's career for him to go beyond the rather narrow scope of his first novel, and in his second work he moves closer to the main-stream of American life. Although it is true that his treatments of war, politics, organized labor, racism, and the plight of the American artist are sometimes shallow, poorly focused, or otherwise marred, his efforts to deal with these topics reflect an expansion of his interests. Artistically, his choice of a panoramic form of novel that could treat a number of characters, each moving in his own milieu and surrounded by his own cast of supporting characters, marks an advance from the techniques of his first novel, as do his increased use of symbolism and his more sophisticated use of time. Clearly, Motley was no longer the predominantly intuitive amateur caught up in the excitement of his own creation; instead, he was becoming a more objective and self-conscious professional who was striving for artistic mastery over a wealth of diverse materials.

CHAPTER 4

Let No Man Write My Epitaph

A S Motley had done after *Knock on Any Door* was published, he left Chicago after the publication of *We Fished All Night* (1951), this time on a pleasure trip. Since he had seen most of the United States in his hobo days and had long been interested in Mexico, he decided to spend a few months touring that country. According to his friend Jack Conroy, Motley already had an idea for his next novel and planned to do some work on it during the vacation.[1] Mexico, however, proved to be more fascinating than Motley had anticipated. After he had visited Mexico City, Cuernavaca, and Puerta Vallarta, he finally bought a house some twelve miles from Mexico City. He remained there for the rest of his life, only occasionally revisiting the United States to renew his tourist card or to take care of business or family matters in Chicago. Although he had always maintained that he had not felt unduly discriminated against in the United States, he told an *Ebony* interviewer in 1958, "Maybe subconsciously I like Mexico because there is a feeling of freedom there. I never think of color until someone brings it up."[2] Ironically, his next novel, written in an environment free of prejudice, dealt more directly with black life in Chicago than had either of his two previous books.

I *A New Professionalism*

By the time Motley began work on his third novel, he had become more professional in his attitude toward his work than he had been at the time he had written the preface to *Knock on Any Door*. There, he insisted that accuracy was his goal and that he had never attempted to make the book "artistic." In public, he always maintained that his art was unconscious and that he knew nothing about style — as in a lecture and the following question and answer period at the University of Wisconsin in 1960.[3] Over the years, however, Motley's insistence that he did not deliberately plan his novels as works of art became a pose to perpetuate his image as proletarian writer.

In reality, his correspondence with his editors and his agents indicates that Motley was well aware of what he was doing and why. During the editing of *Let No Man Write My Epitaph,* problems arose in connection with Motley's use of quotations from popular songs, a technique he had also practiced in his earlier novels. Urged by Hiram Haydn, his editor at Random House, to cut the songs and thereby spare the publisher both the expense of paying for permissions and the trouble of locating some of the copyright holders, Motley replied that the songs were absolutely necessary to achieve the effects for which he had been working. While some songs, such as "I Can See Everybody's Baby" and "As Long as I'm Moving," are used only as a part of the setting, "Mood Indigo" is important to a symbolic pattern that Motley had in mind from the first line of the novel, and he enumerated other examples of songs associated with the symbolism of the work. Defending his use of the song "Cross Over the Bridge," he noted that while the song is blaring over the jukebox in a skidrow bar where Nellie Watkins is drinking, an epileptic is crossing the bridge between control and seizure. This incident foreshadows the bridge that Nellie will cross — to her narcotics dream world — and the bridge that Nick will cross when he sees his mother shooting heroin and realizes that she is an addict.[4] Clearly Motley had planned the symbolism of the novel more carefully than he was willing to admit in interviews.

Motley also insisted on using the exact words he had written, in spite of publishers' worries that some of the terms would be considered indelicate. So firm was his notion of each character that he told Haydn that Frankie Ramponi, a dope pusher, would use no other word but *ass* when instructing Nellie about how to shoot heroin.[5] When Haydn felt that his staff should help Motley eliminate what he felt was accidental awkwardness in certain passages, Motley defended the deliberate crudeness of his style which he sometimes consciously used for its effect.[6] In *We Fished All Night* Motley had been groping for a more artistic expression of his ideas, but in *Let No Man Write My Epitaph* he is more firmly in control of his material and of the means to convey it.

II   *Remembrance of Things Past*

After his disappointing experience with *We Fished All Night,*

Motley attempted to recapture the success he had achieved with *Knock on Any Door.* He did so by creating a character, Nick Romano, Jr., who would retain some of the winning characteristics of Nick while moving in a somewhat different direction, and by developing the character of Louie Romano, who was a small child in *Knock on Any Door.* Together, Nick, Jr., and Louie form a composite of the sort of boy Nick Romano, Sr., could have been under different circumstances.

One other feature of *Epitaph* marks it as a return to Motley's earlier triumph in an even more literal sense. The editing process that *Knock on Any Door* had to undergo before it was printed had resulted in a great deal of cutting that was due, in part, to fear of censorship on the part of his publishers.[7] Now, in addition to telling about the past and quoting sections from the earlier novel to inform those who had not read it, Motley indulged himself by reviewing and rewriting the story of the first Nick Romano's last moments of life. Pages 459 to 463 of *Epitaph* include some of the images that were considered too shocking for a reading audience in 1947, as well as exact details that Motley had obtained in his research concerning the effects of electricity on the human body and the grotesque distortion of a body that has been electrocuted in the electric chair. The execution scene, largely omitted from *Knock on Any Door,* is a strong and effective vignette that adds to the impact of Nick Romano's son's story.

In view of all these ties to *Knock on Any Door, Let No Man Write My Epitaph* may sound like a cynical attempt to cash in on the success of the earlier novel by writing something as nearly like the original as possible. However, Motley felt that in accenting the negative aspects of the tough neighborhood in which the elder Nick Romano grew up, he had presented only one side of slum life as he had perceived it at the time. Throughout his life — in interviews, lectures, and autobiographical articles — Motley insisted that he had found a great deal of compassion and kindness in neighborhoods where, according to the warnings of the middle class people with whom he had grown up, he should have been mugged and robbed if not murdered.[8] In a tragic story such as *Knock on Any Door,* too much emphasis on the good aspects of the slums would have been out of place, although positive characteristics appear from time to time; but in the basically comic novel *Epitaph,* Motley is able to treat the intrinsic nobility of some members of the down and out class with whom he loved to associate.

Consequently, although it is a grim book in many ways and is set in some of the worst neighborhoods of Chicago, although it deals extensively with crime and narcotics addiction, *Let No Man Write My Epitaph* is very different from Motley's first novel in both the tone and the treatment of its materials. Thus, as *Epitaph* moves toward the hopeful resolution associated with comic novels, Motley includes some humorous incidents and picturesque characters whose presence lightens the tone of the entire work. After writing two novels that adhere rather strictly to the basic Naturalistic pattern, he began to modify the literary form to accommodate his changing view of life.

Several basic elements of *Epitaph* had been on Motley's mind for years before he devoted full time to the book. One incident recreates the situation he had treated in "Sister and Brother," written when he was thirteen. Some passages describing the setting are revisions of certain sketches he had published in *Hull-House Magazine* in 1939 and 1940. The early history of Nellie Watkins carries out an intention about which he had written his editor Ted Purdy before the publication of *Knock on Any Door*. Motley had said then that he hoped sometime to do a book about a girl's experience in an orphanage, somewhat similar to Nick's experiences in reform school; he does, however, treat this subject less fully in *Epitaph* than he had originally intended.

In *Knock on Any Door,* Nellie was one of Nick's mistresses and had testified on his behalf despite efforts to browbeat her into testifying for the prosecution. The first few pages of *Let No Man Write My Epitaph* reveal that Nellie had borne a son shortly after Nick's execution, had named him after his illegitimate father, and thought of the baby in almost mystical terms as a reincarnation of the elder Nick: "They took his life and she gave it back."[9] The story opens when Nick, Jr., is five, and Nellie, who is working as a waitress in rundown restaurants on West Madison Street, is doing her best to give her son advantages that she and his father had never had.

In a flashback, Motley sketches Nellie's background in an Iowa orphanage, after she was abandoned by her mother. Like the children in Motley's juvenile piece, "Sister and Brother," Nellie later lived with different relatives, who worked her hard and treated her shabbily. Finally Nellie ran away to Chicago, where she found work as a waitress. The feelings of rootlessness and rejection that naturally stem from this background provide the key to Nellie's character. Feeling unloved, she has been sexually promiscuous from a very early age, first with a boy in the orphanage and then with an uncle, and later with anyone who offered her the slightest warmth, such as the truckdriver who gave her a ride to Chicago. Nick Romano, however, was her most permanent lover, and she showered affection on him, gave him money, waited outside taverns for him, and took him in when he was too drunk to get home. Now that Nick is dead, she romanticizes him as the great love of her life; she has framed the picture that appeared in the newspaper the day he was executed; and she tells herself that Nick really loved her deeply. Nick, Jr., becomes the sole recipient of Nellie's frustrated love; she tries to give him all the affection and tenderness she had missed when she was growing up.

A number of men are important to Nellie and Nick. Judge Edward J. Sullivan, a former circuit court judge, is a dignified elderly gentleman who is nevertheless a "wino." Realizing that it is not good for Nick to grow up in a fatherless household, Nellie often invites the judge to her room to talk with Nick and to give her grammar lessons so that she will be a proper influence on her son. Three young friends of the judge, Max, Phil, and Norman, refer to themselves as Nick's uncles and introduce him to diverse cultural backgrounds: Max is a beer-drinking, fun-loving Mexican American; Phil is a tattoed brawler who has been a member of a Pachuco gang; and Norman is a homosexual. Juan, a friend of Nick's in *Knock on Any Door,* is older and more stable now; he befriends Nellie and becomes young Nick's godfather when he is baptized a Catholic.

Finally, there is Frank Ramponi, a tough Italian narcotics pusher who has all of the elder Nick's good looks and toughness but none of his better qualities. Frank attracts Nellie sexually although she otherwise dislikes him; she does not want him to come in contact with Nick lest he influence the boy. To keep Nellie under his control, Frank introduces her to heroin. Thus, Nellie and other addicts with whom she associates provide the victim's point of view on narcotics traffic in Chicago, while Ramponi exemplifies the profiteering side.

Nick grows up thinking that his mother's gradual disintegration is the result of liquor, and he remains curiously untainted by the tough North Clark Street neighborhood to which they have moved, largely because of his "uncles' " efforts to shield him from many of the harsh facts of life. He is arrested twice because he is often wandering the streets in search of his mother, but his experiences with the police do not cause the kind of bitterness that made his father rebel against society.

At approximately the midpoint of the novel, Motley reintroduces more characters from *Knock on Any Door*. Grant Holloway, by now a wealthy man, is interested in writing a series of articles about drug addiction in the city. Prowling the skid row district in search of material, Grant hears of a boy named Nick Romano and seeks him out. Aunt Rosa discovers the illegitimate son of her dead nephew when Nick's name appears in the paper after his arrest; she pays his fine and introduces him to the rest of the Romano family. The reader discovers what has happened since the end of *Knock on Any Door*: Julian, Nick's brother, was killed in the war; and, as a result of losing both her older sons, Ma Romano is insane. Barren because of the abortion which she begged Nick to arrange, Ang is embittered by her remorse. Louie, who does not know that Nick was executed, looks almost exactly like his brother and is also moving toward a collision with the law. Rosa married late in life, but is the same kindly, cheerful pillar of strength as in the first novel.

Eventually, in spite of the good influences of his uncles, the kindness of the Holloway family, his love for Grant's daughter Barbara, and his artistic ambitions, Nick's depression over Nellie's addiction becomes too much for him to bear. He begins to run around with a tough crowd, smokes marijuana, and graduates to heroin. At about the same time, in a parallel development, a gang war puts Louie in the hospital and then in jail. The balance of the novel traces the salvation of Nick and Louie; one is the literal descendant of Nick Romano, the other, his spiritual reincarnation.

Louie is saved when Aunt Rosa finally tells him that Nick was executed, and he falls in love with Judy, a black waitress. Although their future is uncertain in the book, Motley indicated in a note that he planned a third Romano family novel in which he would deal primarily with their problems in an interracial marriage and with their children.[10] Meanwhile Nick's addiction worsens, leading him to commit several petty crimes. When his uncles hear that he is hooked, however, they raise the money to send him to a federal narcotics clinic in Kentucky. When Nick returns from Kentucky, Sergeant Forbes, a sympathetic narcotics detective, not only helps him to stay off drugs but steals heroin from the police department to give Nellie just enough to stabilize her condition and allow her to lead a nearly normal life. The novel thus ends on a hopeful note.

Unfortunately, Motley's return to the world of Nick Romano did not bring with it the triumph he might have expected. Eleven years had passed since the publication of *Knock on Any Door,* and, as his publishers reminded him, not all potential readers of *Let No Man Write My Epitaph* would have read Motley's first book. David Dempsey, who reviewed the novel for the New York *Times Book Review* and who referred to Nelson Algren, Saul Bellow, and James T. Farrell as Chicago writers in the tradition to which *Epitaph* belongs, mentioned *Knock on Any Door* only parenthetically and even implied that Motley was a latecomer to the Chicago literary scene: "Thus, in a sense, Mr. Motley hoists his trolley after the line has been abandoned. Nothing remains, in this immensely long, crowded and confusing novel about the downtown slum and the society from which it draws its victims, but to turn the screws tighter."[11] Dempsey objected to Motley's treatment of narcotics addiction — the "method of a social worker's case book" — and to the characterization of the judge and Nick's "uncles" and suggested that Motley had imitated O. Henry.

Nelson Algren, an old acquaintance from the Writers' Project days in Chicago, seemed to feel that Motley was poaching on his preserve in writing about dope addicts. Algren, who had published his successful novel *The Man With the Golden Arm* in 1949, must have seemed a logical reviewer to the editors of *Nation;* however, except for some gratuitous insults — the novel is "a syrup that pours too slowly" and Motley "spends most of this one looking for the ball" — Algren has little to say except that he doesn't feel the novel is authentic enough.[12] Motley must have been shocked by the vehemence of Algren's review. The reviewer for *Time* seemed to contrast Motley with Algren. Observing Grant Holloway's practice of using a wire recorder in his research, the reviewer tags Motley with the epithet "The Man with the Wire-Recorder Ear," thus suggesting that Motley is accurate and authentic as a reporter but has not managed to turn his materials into effective fiction, as Algren did in his novel. *Knock on Any Door* is referred to as a modest success, and the latest novel is contrasted with it.[13]

On the other hand, the well-known critic Granville Hicks, who devoted two-thirds of his *Saturday Review* column to *Let No Man Write My Epitaph,* balanced the strengths and weaknesses of the novel much more fairly than the other reviewers had. After noting that the day of Naturalism had been considered long past, he pointed to *Epitaph* as a sign of the continuing vitality of that literary form. Hicks contrasted the "powerful directness" of *Knock on Any Door* to the distractions of the sequel, in which Motley's main faults are his insistence on keeping several themes and plot lines in motion and his use of Holloway as a conveyor of naked statistics about addiction and as a spokesman for Motley himself on life in general. Hicks closed by stating that, as a Naturalist, Motley should dramatize more and disappear "out of sight behind his characters."[14]

Commercially, the novel fared somewhat better than it had with the critics. It sold well at first, though by no means as well as *Knock on Any Door,* but it was selling so poorly by 1963 that Random House renegotiated Motley's royalty arrangement from fifteen to ten percent as a condition for keeping the book in print. *Let No Man Write My Epitaph* appeared in a Signet paperback edition in August 1959; but, according to Random House spokesmen, the novel had not sold enough by mid-1964 to earn its advance. Like Motley's first novel, *Epitaph* attracted the attention of Hollywood and was made into a major movie; however, to Motley's regret, its plot was somewhat streamlined by the screenwriters. The Columbia film introduced James Darren as young Nick, while Shelley Winters (who had won an Oscar the year before as a supporting actress) played Nellie. Ricardo Montalban in the somewhat modified role of Frank Ramponi, Ella Fitzgerald as Big Flora, and Burl Ives as Judge Sullivan were other well-known members of the cast.

In Europe, the novel was better thought of than in the United States. In a 1961 essay about Motley's works, Alfred Weissgarber discounted the unfavorable American reviews and pointed to "Motley's special aptitude . . . his clear perception of the weaknesses, faults, sins, and crimes of Society. . . ."[15] During his lean years in Mexico in the 1960s when his royalties from his American editions were attached by the Internal Revenue Service, Motley still received substantial amounts for the European rights to *Let No Man Write My Epitaph.*[16]

III   *Less Sociology, More Art*

Let No Man Write My Epitaph bears less resemblance to a sociological case history than does *Knock on Any Door;* for, instead of tracing the decline of a single character as he had in his first novel, Motley weaves several story lines into the main plot, each with a number of thematic strands. This technique, utilized rather unsuccessfully in *We Fished All Night,* had become an effective tool by the time he began to write his third novel. In addition to the obvious narcotics theme seized upon by reviewers, several other thematic components enrich the novel. Nick, Jr., and Louie are doubles of each other and are also extensions of the elder Nick Romano, and Motley poses the question of whether they can be saved from the twin menaces of heredity and environment. Nellie's story restates the Naturalist theme of a person doomed by environment as explored in *Knock on Any Door*. The love stories of Nick and Louie comment on separations created and maintained by society. Finally, the minor characters exemplify the basic goodness of even society's discards.

Together, Nick Romano, Jr., and Louie make a composite character who has most of the traits of Motley's earlier creation, Nick Romano. Nick's son bears his father's name and has inherited much of his father's charm. However, unlike the Romano family, preoccupied with survival during the hard times of Nick's youth in Denver and Chicago, Nellie has always put the welfare of her child first; she has reared him carefully according to books on child care, has selected his companions, and has nurtured his artistic and creative impulses. Consequently, instead of turning his ingenuity to outwitting the law as his father did, Nick, Jr., works toward becoming an artist who will interpret the lower depths of society from which he has sprung. That environment is still a threat is made clear by his mother's addiction and by his own trouble with narcotics, but Motley suggests in this novel that it can be overcome: in Nick's case, love and affection at home counteract the effects of the slum life.

Louie Romano comes closer to following the first Nick's example than his nephew does. Louie's uncanny resemblance to Nick, so great that Nellie cannot believe her eyes when she first meets him, suggests that something in the shared heredity of the two brothers has predetermined their destinies. However, the Romano family has changed; for, although money is no longer a problem, a mysterious depression pervades the family. And, like Nick, Louie adds to the troubles of his family. He refuses to consider an honest job and depends instead on money from women who try to buy his affection. Although he is not the real criminal that Nick was, Louie leads young men of his own age into gang fights. Obviously, it is only a matter of time until he will graduate to something more serious.

In Motley's Naturalistic laboratory, then, he examines the inevitability of heredity and environment. The thesis of *Knock on Any Door* is that environment has made a murderer of an innocent altar boy. In the second Romano novel, Motley returns to the setting and the family to test alternatives to his first theory. By sheltering young Nick from some of the worst influences of the street, by providing him with a personal parental attention that Nick, Sr., never had, and by giving him a variety of confidants to whom he can go when he is troubled, Motley arrives at a different set of results. Motley allowed for personal differences by showing that Louie does not react to serious traumata as did his brother. For example, when Louie is shot and jailed, he grows troubled and thoughtful rather than vengeful as Nick always was when he was released from jail. The biggest difference between the brothers, however, is that Louie is able to benefit from Nick's fate. Before his execution, Nick begged Aunt Rosa to make sure his younger brother would not follow his bad example; consequently, after Louie's arrest, Rosa finally tells him what happened to Nick. Motley does not mean to advocate capital punishment as a deterrent to crime, but the fact remains that Nick's tragedy helps Louie reform his life.

Nellie's tragic story is intertwined with the stories of Nick's two counterparts. As both of the young men are on their way to an adjustment of their damaged lives and to victory over their difficulties, Nellie is on her way to defeat. Through her, Motley affirms his earlier tragic vision of the individual who is beaten by a hostile world before he can fight back. From the time she is abandoned in the orphanage, Nellie is programmed for failure. Her story is set beside the more optimistic lives of Nick, Jr., and Louie as a reminder to the reader of the usual effects of unfavorable environments on children. The many examples provided by Nellie's addicted friends also show that Motley is not backing away from the basic conclusions he had reached when he was writing *Knock on Any Door*; he is simply qualifying them by making allowances for individual cases.

The love stories of the principal characters are related thematically and provide a unifying element for the divergent plot lines. Nick's death at the hands of society separated Nellie from her lover, a fact of which the reader is frequently reminded. Louie is also separated from Judy by society, since society proscribes interracial love affairs and marriages; and Nick, Jr., and Barbara Holloway are separated by the differences in their economic and social backgrounds. It is worth noting that, in spite of the individual's determination not to be influenced by society's edicts, he finds it difficult to triumph over the accumulated prejudices that separate race from race and class from class.

Louie and Judy are personally capable of transcending the barriers of race, but they must live in a world that considers racial classification extremely important. Grant Holloway has instilled democratic attitudes in his daughter, who sees no significant obstacle between her and Nick; but Nick himself is awed by the difference in backgrounds, and Barbara's mother is deeply disturbed by her daughter's relationship with an illegitimate slum boy whose mother is a "junkie" and whose father died in the electric chair. At the end of the novel, Louie is still trying to find Judy, who is deliberately avoiding him; and Nick has promised Grant that he will not see Barbara until he has been free of narcotics for a year. Thus, Motley leaves their futures in doubt — in itself a hopeful stance compared with the usual Naturalistic tendency to end novels with explicit tragedies.

Another feature that tempers the grim Naturalistic treatment of the novel's main theme is Motley's insistence on the essential goodness of most people — even in the tough slums around West Madison Street — as exemplified in his creation of minor characters such as the judge and Nick's uncles. While the depiction of minor criminals and prostitutes with hearts of gold may remind the reader of the sentimental flaws in the works of Bret Harte and O. Henry, he must remember that Motley lived close to the people whose lives he is describing. Soon after moving to his basement apartment near the Maxwell Street market, Motley wrote his *Hull-House Magazine* vignettes about the honesty and kind-heartedness of the area's inhabitants — how they did not steal from the open pushcarts and how they replaced the money lost by a young girl. Whatever the reaction of the critics, Motley intended to make the point that is so explicitly enunciated by Grant Holloway: "The dirty end of the stick.... That's what Society handed them.... And they're not completely bad. Jesus Christ, no! There's something decent in every one of them" (406).

In fairness to Motley, it should be acknowledged that he does not ignore the sordid side of his characters' lives. While Judge Sullivan is kind to Nick and Nellie and while his appearance and behavior reflect his upper class origin, Motley never lets us forget that he is an alcoholic. When he and Nick's uncles are saving money to buy

Nick an electric train for Christmas, Sullivan is not above borrowing the price of a drink from the money that he holds for the group. Unflattering aspects of Nick's uncles are ironically most evident when they collect money to cure Nick's heroin addiction: Max combines his cab driving with part-time work as a panderer, Phil prostitutes himself to homosexuals, and Norm blackmails his own father. Sentimental scenes like the Christmas party are balanced by grim episodes such as Frank Ramponi's murder. When Frank, jealous of Nellie's affection for her son, beats Nick, Max and Juan decide to kill Ramponi. They borrow a .45 automatic and take turns carrying it as they wait to encounter Frank in the neighborhood. They fail to kill him only because Frank's former partner kills him first.

The introduction of other themes does not diminish the importance of the attack that Motley launches upon narcotics and those who sell them. In *Let No Man Write My Epitaph,* dope is presented as a corrupting influence on mankind, the equivalent of law and the penal system in *Knock on Any Door.* A good index of the degenerative effect of narcotics is seen in Nellie's evolution from a devoted mother to a selfish addict whose only preoccupation is her next fix. Ramponi, the pusher who introduces Nellie to heroin to gain control over her, is one of Motley's few real villains, a criminal with no redeeming virtues. Unlike Nick, Sr., a good boy driven to a life of crime, Ramponi enjoys living outside the law. He profits handsomely from his customers while keeping clear of hard drugs himself, and he apparently participates in other crimes like armed robbery for the stimulation they offer. Although Motley has often sympathized with criminals in the past and condones the breaking of certain laws even in *Epitaph,* the author clearly has no sympathy for Frankie's cold and calculating type of crime. Significantly, Motley indicates that corruption in other areas of society facilitates the dope trade by showing how Don Lockwood, the politician who first appeared in *We Fished All Night,* arranges to protect pushers in return for a share of the profits.

Faced with the problem of introducing a great deal of documentary material into the novel, a problem shared by most Naturalistic writers, Motley employs a variety of methods, the least effective being the undramatized recitation of the facts of narcotics addiction. An example is Chapter 37 in which Motley produces what amounts to a brief essay on fear among addicts by detailing the hazards that threaten them: "Fear is what rules them. They are afraid of the police. The sheriff's force. Of running out of money.

Of having to kick it, cold turkey, in jail. Of getting a hot shot. Of being caught with it on them — possession — a one- to five-year sentence. Of an overdose" (164). Besides these dangers, there is the normal fear of just not getting enough heroin to keep from "getting sick," from being stricken with withdrawal symptoms. Motley details the desperate efforts of the junkies to stay ahead of their habits by prostituting themselves or by becoming dope peddlers in turn. Some cheat other junkies, selling "frosted" capsules (ones that appear to be full of heroin but are actually half empty), or by selling heroin that has been diluted by each middleman through whose hands it has passed.

While it may have appeared to the unsympathetic critic that in such chapters Motley was simply indulging in sensational journalism, even in these he remains the novelist. He alternates the clinical language of a sociological report with the colloquial language of the addicts and pushers themselves, just as he alternates from objective third person narration to the greater immediacy of second person: "Say you need some real bad and somebody gave you a bad lot and you struck yourself with it. You'd know right away. When you hit yourself with it you'd know it wasn't any good" (165). He conveys not only his point but also the ways of thinking, speaking, and feeling that prevail in the drug culture.

Another aspect of Motley's attack on narcotics requires the use of an outsider whose lack of involvement and whose ignorance of the drug scene make him the representative of the novel's average reader. Thus, one of Motley's reasons for reintroducing Grant Holloway is that his experiences are, to some extent, intended to parallel the reader's own growing awareness. First, Grant gets the bare facts for his articles through library research. Second, he supplements cold statistics with the personal histories and knowledge of people who are close to the problem: Juan, who is in love with one junkie and who sees scores of others daily; Sergeant Bill Forbes of the narcotics division; and Marty Cavanaugh, sheriff of Cook County. Third, Grant personally encounters an addict when he meets Nellie. His growing pity, revulsion, and sense of outrage at the destruction caused by narcotics are certainly reflections of Motley's own feelings, and thus lead to the charge that Grant is simply a spokesman for his creator; more important, however, is the fact that Grant Holloway reacts the way Motley hopes the reader will.

But sympathy and understanding are not enough. Motley offers constructive advice as well: he wants to show how a bit of training

in sociology plus a bit of compassion can result in a better approach
to the narcotics problem; how, instead of allowing the pushers to
buy safety while they crack down on the addicts, law enforcement
agencies should punish the pusher and treat the addict with humanity. Sergeant Forbes, who is the embodiment of this concept, is an
honest cop who has requested a narcotics assignment as the result
of his pity for the victims of narcotics, the addicts he often had to
arrest on his beat. Besides serving as a source of information for
Grant, Forbes is connected to the main plot by his encounters with
Nick and Nellie. During one drug raid, he allows Nick to escape
because of his youth and his pathetic "abandoned" appearance;
and he later makes the arrangements for Nick to enter the federal
clinic to be cured. Finally, recognizing Nellie as incurable, he supplies her with free drugs so that she does not have to resort to
prostitution for money to satisfy her habit. As the epitome of the
humane and enlightened policeman, Forbes is perhaps intended to
balance the tough, sadistic cops in Motley's first novel; but he is
not a completely successful character because he is simply too good
to be true.

Motley attempted to counteract the sociological approach to the
narcotics plot with a greater use of symbolism than in his two previous novels. To the dismay of his publishers, who had to worry
about copyright arrangements and royalties, Motley always insisted
on using popular songs in order to recreate the atmosphere of the
times, much as John Dos Passos had done with newspaper headlines. Especially in *We Fished All Night,* where he employed songs
such as "We're Gonna Have to Slap the Dirty Little Jap," "Der
Fuehrer's Face," and "Praise the Lord and Pass the Ammunition,"
Motley used this technique rather straightforwardly. However,
even as early as *Knock on Any Door,* he had seen other possibilities
for using songs, for he had achieved a nice irony by beginning the
brief and tragic love affair between Nick and Emma with the song
"Always." Similarly in *We Fished All Night,* the song "Route 66"
with its repeated line "get your kicks" serves as a commentary on
the war stories told by ex-servicemen.

In *Let No Man Write My Epitaph,* Motley again uses songs for
background; for example, "I Can See Everybody's Baby" and "As
Long as I'm Movin' " capture the atmosphere of a black bar. But
the author exploits the symbolic values of the songs more extensively than he had before. While Nellie relives her early life as an
unwanted and unloved child and as the unappreciated mistress of

Nick Romano, the jukebox in the bar appropriately plays "Mood Indigo." Later in the novel, the same lyrics provide a counterpoint to the excruciating process of withdrawal that Nick undergoes in the federal institution. "You Are My Sunshine," another of Nellie's favorite songs, is consciously associated with the warmth that Nick, Jr., brings into her life. Louie Romano adopts "One for My Baby" as a correlative for his loss of Judy toward the end of the novel. Motley's use of the song "Cross Over the Bridge" to signal Nick's discovery of his mother's addiction has been mentioned earlier as a more complex symbolic use of music. Another notable song is "ABC Boogie," whose innocent title and lyrics are an ironic background for a teenage party attended by young Nick. While the phonograph repeats lyrics about students learning "readin', writin', a-rith-me-tic," Nick's classmates are educating each other in the less wholesome aspects of sex and drugs: "They shot themselves, those who were that advanced. All of them, the weedheads and the hypos, lay around in all sorts of positions on the floor and on couches, talking, taking off, feeling fine, dozing down" (436).

Motley also used a more deliberate pattern of color symbolism in *Epitaph* than in any of his previous novels. The principal key colors are yellow, white, sky blue, and blue-black. In the first scene of the novel, young Nick stands at the top of a hill in the yellow sunshine, looking down at a field of yellow dandelions. The sky above him is "bluer than his blue crayon" (3) and is devoid of clouds. The gaiety of the colors, in conjunction with the fresh smells of the outdoors and the feeling of the unfamiliar long grass against his ankles, suggests a freedom and happiness that are soon to vanish. Nick and Nellie are at a Wisconsin resort maintained by a charitable organization for the benefit of the underprivileged, but society's attempt to help is a fleeting gesture, whose transitory nature (and the transitory nature of all life) is underscored symbolically on the second page of the novel. Nellie shows Nick that some of the dandelions have turned white, "that just like people all the dandelions got gray hair when they were old" (4). White, or sometimes gray, becomes a symbol of death and loss, most notably in the white powder of heroin that causes Nellie to age prematurely. The bright blue of the Wisconsin sky vanishes as Nick and Nellie return to Chicago; in its place is the blue-black of the West Madison Street night, which Motley personifies as a blue-black panther, stalking its many victims. This blue-black is related to the "Mood Indigo," which grips Nellie on her return to the city, in a knitting together of song and color symbolism.

These colors — blue and yellow holding out hope for Nick while
white and blue-black threaten him — are woven throughout the
novel. Blue and yellow are the colors with which Nick creates a
world of his own when he draws pictures with crayons: blue skies
and the blue of Lake Michigan cheer Nick when he is troubled; the
yellow of a neighbor's canary, glimpsed through her window, suggests that the new neighborhood to which he and his mother move
will be safer and happier. The yellow and gold of the sun are used
similarly, in opposition to the ominous quality of Chicago's blue-
black night. On one occasion Frank Ramponi, always associated
with the dark side of Chicago life, symbolically destroys Nick's
happiness when he callously swats a yellow and black bee that Nick
is watching.

Personification of the city and its abstract forces is another technique Motley uses to transcend the merely sociological approach:
Chicago is sometimes a blue-black panther, sometimes a pimp,
sometimes a whore with "painted face and dirty underwear" (185).
When Nellie first arrives in Chicago, she is frightened by "the great
beast of a city. It was at the moment eating its young and its
old. . . . It was like a blue-black beast in the night. Its eyes, neon,
were cat eyes in the dark. . . . Its bare feet in the mud, toenails
black and broken. And the heavy breathing of an animal asleep but
its cat eyes open" (34–35).

On the other hand, West Madison Street can sometimes appear
as innocuous as a clown with a painted face; elsewhere, it is per-
sonified as vicious but cowardly, a cur with its tail between its legs,
afraid to attack any but the weak (181). North Clark Street seems
more suave, perhaps because it is near "the good places" in
Chicago; but it is more corrupt than West Madison:

> North Clark Street is a hustler, hard-eyed, little mustache preened. He's
> got to have what you have or he won't sleep tonight.
> He's got connections. Whore you want? Cheap whore? Fancy, high-
> class call girl? Drugs you want? Your own sex you want? Anything you
> want.
> He's got connections.
> He's the hustler, the con-man, the pimp. The guy you have to look out
> for. (181)

Motley continues the personification for almost a page before he caps the description with his most vivid metaphor: "If [North Clark Street] were a woman he would be a diseased prostitute sitting there picking her open sores in public" (182).

Finally, though not precisely symbolic, the title itself, which Motley insisted on using despite the objections of his Random House editors, has an extended meaning. Taken from the speech of Robert Emmett, an Irish rebel convicted of treason in the early nineteenth century, the title emphasizes the immense gap between the underworld of Motley's Chicago and the world of his readers. Motley quotes Emmett as saying, "No man can write my epitaph.... Let my character and motives repose in obscurity and peace, till other times and other men can do them justice" ([vii]). The novel ends with two italicized lines: *"Nellie? Nick the father? Nick the son? / Let no man write their epitaph"* (467). Thus, Motley indicates that no man is capable of judging his three characters, for they have had to live a life so far removed from the sphere of the average reader that conventional rules of morality seem inadequate.

IV   *Black Characters*

In his third published novel, Motley at last came to grips with black characters. Robert Bone, who has accused Motley of deliberately avoiding black life "as a matter of principle," suggests that his use of white protagonists hints at a deep psychological conflict.[17] However, Motley's own background was hardly typical of the black experience in America; and, although he had occasionally suffered racial insults and rebuffs, he knew far less about black ghetto life than about life in the racially mixed neighborhood where he had grown up. Like Jean Toomer, Motley had to make a conscious effort to establish ties with black culture. Moreover, Bone's comments are based only on the first two novels, in which Motley did not cast blacks in important roles. In *Knock on Any Door* there are brief glimpses of black characters in the Colorado reform school, and a single incident of racial bigotry occurs when Bricktop orders a new black prisoner to be segregated by the other boys. Sunshine, one of Nick's Chicago friends, is drawn almost as a caricature: "His brown, almost black face was shiny, greasy-looking on his forehead, on his cheekbones and across his flat nose. His kinky hair stood up all over his head and was in a tall cockscomb just at the front. His lips were pushed out in a sad pout."[18]

The ironically named Sunshine is often the butt of jokes, but he shows unexpected strength when he repays Nick's friendship by attempting to lie for him on the witness stand during the murder trial. In spite of his crucial testimony, however, Sunshine is a very minor figure in the novel. Equally insignificant is Dave Wilson in *We Fished All Night,* although according to Motley's original plan for "Of Night, Perchance of Death," Wilson was to have been an important and complex character.

In *Let No Man Write My Epitaph,* on the other hand, black characters are much more in evidence, and one woman, Judy, plays a key role in the novel. Louie Romano encounters her in the tearoom where she works as a waitress and is immediately attracted to her. Unlike every other girl he has ever wanted, Judy refuses to tumble into bed with him; in fact, she refuses to talk to him for some time, assuming that he is simply a white lecher trying to "change his luck" by sleeping with a black girl. He persists until Judy dates him; ultimately they fall deeply in love. Motley contrasts Louie's reception by the black world with Judy's treatment in the white world. When Louie takes Judy to his home for dinner, surprising his family by not telling them of her race in advance, even Aunt Rosa and Rosemary are taken aback and behave awkwardly. The family is polite, although Ang inwardly seethes with hatred and exaggerated shame that her brother would date and perhaps plan to marry a black woman.

In another incident Motley explores the cliché about mixed couples being anathema to both races. In a black night club on the South Side, Louie is observed with interest by some of the women, but one man reacts with hostility: "At the table behind them a young Negro sat alone. Drunk, or only angry, he said, loud enough for them to hear, '. . .white.' And a little later, '. . .white bastard,' just loud enough for them to hear. He was on his home field, in his own ball park. He had been pushed around in theirs" (386). Judy quiets the young man and avoids a fight by telling him that Louie is "colored just like us," but she implies that he is simply light enough to pass for white. Immediately the young man apologizes profusely. By showing how readily the white man can pass for black, Motley suggests that the black world is more tolerant than white society.

Besides Judy, who is from a respectable family and knows nothing of the Chicago underworld, Motley creates an interesting gallery of black characters in the drug subculture he presents. To narcotics addicts, race is of no significance, for black and white borrow and share their supplies in a harmony that puts the "square" world to shame. Realizing that they are all afflicted by the same terrible problem, heroin users treat one another with sympathy and understanding, as does Big Florabelle: "Florabelle because she was born in the Deep South. Big because she was just that. Big and fat. Almost as wide as she was tall. Black. Good-natured, always laughing, ready to lend a stranger a dollar in exchange for a hard-luck story. She knew you five minutes and she'd give her life for you" (96).

Big Florabelle hangs out in a bar frequented by other black junkies, including Joe Brown, known as Big Black on the street. He has won the title from Charlie Collins, or Little Black, when each humorously claimed to be the blackest man in the neighborhood, but both were superceded when Extra Black Johnson came to town. Good-bye George is a young man who wants to go back to Tennessee but who invariably spends his savings on liquor. Associating with this group is "Uncle Sam," a nineteen year old white who prefers to shoot his heroin among blacks rather than whites. On the fringes of the group is Fran, the beautiful young junkie whose hopeless affair with Nick's friend Juan provides a counterpoint to the interracial romance between Louie and Judy.

Like some writers of the Harlem Renaissance thirty years earlier, Motley sketches a few of the exotic primitive scenes that his white readers expect. For example, Grant and a white friend are in the Maxwell Street secondhand shop Juan owns:

Outside the window had now come the Sunday sidewalk church meeting: a group of Negroes of various colors, sizes and shapes. Some beat tambourines, others clap their hands together. There is a woman preacher, a big black woman, built like a man and dressed in a purple hat with a white plume, a blue satin dress and pink shoes. *Let the Loooord bleeesss you-all!* ... The little group claps hands in rhythm. Their eyes are frantic. Their hands are frantic. Their feet hop like drumsticks against the sidewalk. (214)

For the most part, however, Motley uses scenes of black life only when they can add to the development of themes or characters and not merely for local color as in the preceding passage. Above all, he remains an integrationist, both in emphasizing the breakdown of racial barriers among the heroin addicts and in the interracial romance that saves Louie from his older brother's fate.

V   *Not an Epitaph*

The publication of *Let No Man Write My Epitaph* marked an upward turn in the career of Willard Motley. The failure of *We Fished All Night* in 1951 had made it appear that Motley's first book had been a sort of lucky accident, that he had been a one book novelist who had insisted on writing a second novel. However, the lessons he had learned in writing the unsuccessful second work resulted in a third novel that displayed a more sophisticated handling of social problems than had the best seller of the 1940s.

We Fished All Night, Motley's halting attempt to produce a panoramic novel rather than a story centered on one individual, had taught him to weave together the strands of several plots — to relate subsidiary themes to his main theme so that the fate of the principal character does not stand alone as an unrelated event. Furthermore, employing both Nick Romano, Jr., and Louie Romano as protagonists who complement one another adds a kind of strength to *Epitaph* that *Knock on Any Door* does not have. In the earlier book, Nick's tie to the mass of underprivileged youth had to be asserted by a spokesman or by the narrator, but the implications of *Epitaph* emerge more naturally from the drama of the novel. Thus, *Let No Man Write My Epitaph* indicated the continuing vitality and artistic development of its creator.

Ironically, although in some ways it was a more mature artistic effort than Motley's first novel, *Let No Man Write My Epitaph* has a poorer chance of attaining a lasting place in American literary history. Granville Hicks was right when he noted that the second Romano book did not have the intensity of the first. The reason is clear when one considers Motley's deep personal involvement in the real life counterparts of the characters in *Knock on Any Door.* On the other hand, while he had known people like those in *Epitaph,* he had never invested as much emotional commitment in any single individual as he had in the two prototypes of the first Nick Romano. In the sequel he relied far less heavily on direct personal experience and more heavily on invention. Like Dreiser, Motley wrote best when he emphasized not art but emotion — when he drew heavily upon his own experiences and the experiences of those closest to him.

CHAPTER 5

Let Noon Be Fair

A S Motley became more familiar with his adopted country and
more detached from his native Chicago, he began to see literary material in Mexico. He developed a great deal of love and
respect for the Mexican people, and he formed a close personal tie
by taking two young Mexican boys, Raul and Sergio, into his
home; he dedicated *Let No Man Write My Epitaph* to Sergio. By
1961, when Jack Conroy visited him, Motley was making plans for
a novel set in Mexico, supposedly "a placid, good-humored and
humorous novel" that would have been quite different from anything he had ever written.[1] However, as time passed, Motley's conception of the book changed, either because of pressure from his
publishers or because of his own inclination toward fiction that was
critical of society.

His early plans did result in a pleasant nonfiction book that deals
with his personal experiences and observations; this significant
work, "My House Is Your House," is discussed in Chapter Six.
Robert Loomis of Random House rejected "My House," and Motley, already irritated by arguments over relatively trivial problems
in the publication of *Let No Man Write My Epitaph,* decided to
seek a new publisher. G. P. Putnam's Sons expressed interest in
"My House" as well as in Motley's projected Mexican novel, but,
except for a few chapters that appeared in *Rogue,* a men's magazine, "My House Is Your House" was never published. The novel
with the working title "Tourist Town" was the main fruit of his
thirteen year sojourn in Mexico, and it was undergoing revision
when Motley died. Published by G. P. Putnam, *Let Noon Be Fair*
appeared less than a year after his death.

I   *Typecasting an Author?*

As early as January 1957, Motley had conceived the book that

109

was to be his last work. A note written during that month sketches the framing passages that Motley planned to use to unify the work; for, without this rather artificial envelope structure, he feared that the work would seem too episodic. The novel was to open in a hospital in which a prize-winning novelist is lying close to death after an auto accident. He and his two sons — one natural, one adopted — expect that he will die. The injured man reveals that he has never cared for his natural son, who reminds him of his unhappy marriage, and that his adopted son has been his real favorite. He asks his adopted son, who also wants to be a writer, to finish his novel about a small Mexican village that is overrun by American tourists and is losing its original character; this son finishes the novel, which forms the bulk of the book. In a closing passage, the father was to recover and publish the book. Motley stayed with this plan to the point of writing the framing chapters and submitting them to Putnam's, but the sections were wisely omitted from the published version of the novel.

Disagreements over the appropriateness of these contrived and sentimental framing chapters were only the first of many difficulties Motley was to have with the new book. He had hoped to be able to work in harmony with his new publisher; however, after parts of his manuscript had been received at Putnam's, it became evident that he and his editor would have conflicting opinions about many aspects of the Mexican novel. As a best-selling author, Motley had evidently been considered a prize when he came to Putnam's because Peter Israel, editor in chief of the publishing house, handled the correspondence with Motley personally. In his letters to Motley, Israel raised numerous objections.[2] He was concerned about the unsympathetic depiction of nearly all the "gringos" contrasted with what he felt was an overly favorable treatment of the Mexicans. To Israel, Motley was oversimplifying the complex conflict between the cultures into a basic conflict between good and evil. Ironically, he also felt that Motley, who had been threatened with censorship so often in the past, was becoming timid and was toning down material that could result in another best seller. He urged Motley to write a tough, explicit book, something that Motley had always done in the past despite the objections of his publishers. A final irony was Israel's concern that the book would not be as long as Motley had estimated. Motley, who had always had to cut his manuscripts drastically, must have felt that his world was turned upside down.

Hiding the anger and bitterness evoked by Israel's letters, Motley wrote long letters of explanation and summaries of what he intended to do in future chapters of "Tourist Town," and he also pointed out that his planned revisions would eliminate many of the publisher's objections. Warning Israel politely that too early criticism could be damaging, Motley stated that he would prefer to wait until his entire first draft was completed before being confronted with any demands or suggestions from Putnam's.[3] Privately, however, he complained irritably to some of his friends that he felt the publishing house was behaving as if he were a mere beginner, for it was giving him his advance money in installments as each section of the novel was submitted.

In a letter to John Dodds, of the McIntosh-McKee Agency, he criticized this practice and pointed out that he had had two novels made into movies and three reprinted by paperback publishing houses. The fact that the Dodds letter was written the same day that Motley sent a reasonable, unargumentative letter to Israel suggests that Motley felt he was being treated badly but knew that he was in no position to argue because of his financial troubles.[4] Israel occasionally rubbed salt into the wounds — perhaps unwittingly — by referring to the one thousand dollar advance installments as having been paid against his better judgment and by threatening to make no more payments until the book was completed.

Motley's journal for the 1960s shows that he was in dire need of money. Because of his relative naiveté regarding business matters and taxes, his income was interrupted by the Internal Revenue Service, which attached more than one thousand dollars collected by Motley's agents, royalties for *Knock on Any Door,* in October 1963. Motley was still in debt for his house outside Mexico City, and he desperately attempted to keep some funds coming in by having money for foreign rights sent directly to him in Mexico. When advance payments from Putnam's did not arrive on time, Motley even questioned whether he should spend a few centavos for bus fare to his bank; he feared that if the money did not come, he would be just that much closer to starvation. The publication *Rogue* became a major source of income, as it paid him $350 for each of four chapters of "My House Is Your House" that were printed as articles in 1964 and 1965. The one hundred dollars the Chicago *Sun-Times* paid for his autobiographical essay "Some Thoughts on Color" was welcome.

Even Motley's days in the slums of Chicago during the Depres-

sion had not been so desperate. It is possible that his extreme poverty caused Motley to delay seeking the medical aid that might have
saved his life.[5] Yet, in spite of his real need for money during the
early 1960s, when Felix Pollack, curator of the rare book room at
the University of Wisconsin, asked Motley for his papers for the
library's collection, the author brushed aside an offer of payment
and donated his papers covering the years 1957 to 1963, a gesture
that epitomizes the generosity so characteristic of the man.

Surprisingly, Motley's creative faculties seem to have reacted
well to the adversity, for representative entries in his journal record
his output in late 1964 as being more than respectable. On November 21, he produced forty-eight handwritten pages, which he estimated would come to about twenty-four typed pages. On November 25, he wrote forty-four pages by hand; on November 26,
sixteen pages; on November 27, thirty-three pages; on November
29, forty-three pages. So involved was he in the new novel that he
sometimes could not sleep, as on the night of December 9, 1964,
when he had to get up a number of times to write down things that
he had thought of after retiring.

In spite of Israel's repeated objections and suggestions, Motley
forged ahead with the first draft; he hoped to be able to argue for
his concept of the novel when the entire book was completed.
Unfortunately, his sudden death left the unrevised manuscript in
the hands of his publishers, who had paid a sizable cash advance
for it. Unlike his earlier novels, which had been revised by Motley
in conference with his publishers' editorial staffs, his last book was
edited by others and printed in 1966 as *Let Noon Be Fair*. While
some obvious weaknesses such as the framing passages were
excised, the book is probably less successful than it would have
been if Motley had been alive to supervise its final editing.

II   *The Story of a Tourist Town*

Let Noon Be Fair details the gradual erosion of a town's moral
standards and the loss of its older Mexican culture to the garish
coney island atmosphere that "developers" create for American
tourists. The story of the town is told for the most part through the
stories of individuals and families whose varied reactions to the
changes in Las Casas give meaning to the fate of the town itself.
Motley uses both flat and rounded characters, a fact that most
reviewers failed to recognize. Many of the American tourists, as

critics noted, blend into each other to form a group of stereotypes such as the bored middle-aged man or woman who is seeking sexual adventure, the homosexual who is indulging appetites he dares not satisfy at home, or the "wheeler-dealer" who is hoping to make a fast dollar and move on. Such characters, who often appear only briefly, are generally not fully developed and seem in some cases to have been deliberately designed as copies of one another. Motley told Peter Israel that his intention was to show such tourists up as monied "vagabonds" who drift from place to place seeking amusement.[6] Motley never intended that these flat figures would have the depth of his more completely rounded characters, who compose the second type: several Americans and many Mexicans who have continuing roles in the novel; they adjust, grow, or go down to defeat as the town's nature changes.

As the novel opens, the leading family in Las Casas is the Espinoza family, whose prestige stems from the fact that they are Spanish and not Mexican. The patriarch of the Espinozas, who owns property in Spain, in Mexico City, and in Las Casas, serves as a sort of symbolic representative of the conquistadores who invaded and exploited Mexico in the sixteenth century. Sophisticated and regal, Espinoza seems to have life under control, but life deals ironically with him. His son Silvio, who must carry on the family line, is a chinless weakling dominated by his wife Florencia, who defies Spanish tradition by refusing to bear him more children after their first child Juana is born deformed. Silvio loses himself in alcohol, and is occasionally courageous enough to beat Florencia.

After the deformed child is given to a servant whose own baby has been born dead, the only member of the family who acknowledges the child's existence, the elder Espinoza, pathetically follows her, feeds her candy, and plays with her. The child, Juana, becomes a town character; feeble-minded and grotesque (she eventually weighs two hundred pounds and stands nearly six feet tall), she is taunted by other children, who call her "La Luchadora," the wrestler. The history of these three generations of Spanish aristocracy provides a microcosmic parallel to the decline of Spanish influence in the Mexican town.

A second major family in Las Casas is that of Hector Beltran, the richest man in town, who has also been frustrated by fate. He has four daughters but no son to perpetuate his dynasty. He compensates by building schools, banks, and stores that bear his name and by lavishing his affection on his most beautiful and intelligent daughter, Paz. Unfortunately, Paz discovers that the Beltran fortune was acquired by swindling illiterate Indians out of their land. Because she has loved her father so deeply, she reacts by hurting him as badly as she can: to atone for his sins, she will renounce life and enter a convent. Although Beltran forbids her name to be spoken in his house, he secretly carries her picture and reads her letters. After years in the convent Paz realizes that she had acted out of vindictiveness and not from religious sentiment. But she has been divorced from the outside world for too long; her mother tells her that she must stay in the convent. Don Hector builds a hospital in her name and then tries to transfer his hopes to Soledad, his youngest. As if to renew the vitality in the family's blood — or perhaps to atone for its sins — Soledad marries Gustavo, son of a hotel cook from Indian stock. As Beltran's surrogate son, Gustavo becomes a shrewd and ruthless businessman; and, when Don Hector dies, futilely asking for Paz, the family is richer than ever.

The third principal family is that of Tizoc, an Indian peasant who boasts that he can neither read nor write. Beltran's rival for leadership of the town, Tizoc also got his start as a thief, although with more mitigating circumstances than Beltran had. As a boy, Tizoc had worked in a monastery where he had observed the monks growing fat on the contributions of the poor. Learning from this example, Tizoc began to steal from his masters; and, when the monks fled the monastery during the revolution, twenty-two year old Tizoc seized the opportunity to steal seven burro loads of property from the church. He later uses the stolen money to buy the trucking line that serves Las Casas and takes advantage of his monopoly by charging high freight rates. His wife, foreshadowing the American domination to come, orders furniture, china, and clothes from Montgomery Ward and serves foods imported from the United States. But neither his money nor his succession of "gringa" mistresses can compensate Tizoc for his children's lack of love for him.

His daughter Yolanda tries to rebel against his authority by sleeping with most of the young men in town, but Tizoc is immune to embarrassment. Leaving her illegitimate son to her lover, Mario Serrano, Yolanda eventually marries an American salesman whom Tizoc establishes as manager of an American style hotel. Tizoc's sons, Faustino and Francisco, are less like their father than his money-making son-in-law. Faustino, a playboy, wastes money as fast as Tizoc can provide it; and serious and bookish Francisco feels contempt for his father's crude materialism.

Two other important characters are linked by a long-standing sexual liaison. Although he seems to love María Camacho, Juan Campos becomes a priest, largely in order to enjoy an idle, luxurious life. María responds by making an equally practical economic decision: she goes to work at the small, run-down whorehouse in Las Casas; and, when the elderly madame dies, she runs it with a flair that causes the house to become a landmark, a must on every male tourist's list of attractions. María lends her profits from the brothel at high rates of interest and becomes wealthy.

Father Campos has similar good fortune within the church, for he soon takes over as pastor in Las Casas. A parasite on the townspeople, he indulges his appetites for rich foods, imported wines — and María. María allows herself to become pregnant by Father Campos, apparently because she both wants a child and wishes Campos to have a constant reminder of his hypocrisy. Because of the child Carlos, María sells her house and opens a respectable hotel. Surprisingly, Carlos is quite religious until he becomes aware that the clergy extort the few assets of the poor. Then the young man rebels against the church and tries to convince people to use their money to feed their children.

Most sympathetically treated of the principal Mexican families are the Serranos. Mario is virtually the only member of his generation who resists the corruption that comes with the American tourists. Although he falls in love with Cathy Mathews, a "gringa" who becomes a permanent resident of the town, he remains true to himself by living as he wishes. In this way he is like his father, a fisherman who has been the village freethinker. Mario's father, who refused to let the priests take advantage of him, thus became a man of some substance through his own hard work. Because Mario inculcates similar values in his own (and Yolanda's) son, the Serrano family holds out a frail hope that some Mexicans may be able to retain their integrity in spite of the American invasion. Mario, who launches a deliberate counterattack on the developers, finally refuses to sell his beach property and thereby blocks the construction of a major resort. Similarly unmaterialistic, his son Elmundo (whose name significantly translates as "the world") transcends the increasing unpleasantness of his surroundings by becoming an artist.

These sketches of the chief Mexican characters in the novel should serve to counter one of the major complaints expressed by

Motley's editor and by some reviewers — that Motley treated the Mexicans too sympathetically and the Americans too harshly. From the beginning, he had planned to show that veins of corruption run through the native population; that corruption is intensified, not introduced, by the Americans. The other side of this complaint — that Motley was too harsh in his treatment of the *norteamericanos* — should be judged by the continuing American characters, those present throughout most of the novel, rather than by those who appear only briefly.

Tom Van Pelt is one of the first Americans to discover Las Casas. Like Motley, he comes from Chicago and is an author; although he is not black, he is something of an outsider, an onlooker rather than a participant in the life of the American colony. His role is symbolized by his habit of sitting on his balcony and observing events. Tom is frequently ashamed of his countrymen, and although he remains even after the Americanization of the town, he regrets the passing of the small fishing village he has known. Tom's apartment, or his table in the local cafe or tavern, always serves as a nucleus for the American visitors who are willing to respect their hosts: to observe customs without ridiculing or attempting to change them, to live in harmony with the Mexicans, and to leave the town as they found it. Tom is friendly with Mario's father and later with Mario, and when the third generation, that of Elmundo, grows up, the teenage boys make Tom their confidant. Standing between two cultures, he understands better than anyone else the changes that threaten the Mexican town.

Another sympathetic American is Cathy Mathews, who came to Las Casas with her husband; early prototypes of the tourists who will later inundate the village, they marvel at the low prices and exclaim over the quaint customs. However, after Bob deserts Cathy, she becomes a true resident of the town; she starts a school to teach English as well as reading and writing in Spanish, and she organizes a group to build a library. Like Van Pelt, she serves as a conscience for the American presence in the town, observing many of the crude actions of fellow Americans and helping the Mexicans to fight against exploitation. She also opposes the traditional power of the Catholic church and of Father Campos by speaking out for birth control and against censorship and by attempting to better the living conditions of the poor and to broaden the horizons of the children.

Less appealing than Tom or Cathy are the wealthy Whitehorns, other long-term residents of Las Casas. Harold Whitehorn plays at being a painter, while his wife makes a career out of brow-beating the servants. Their son Hal, however, thinks of himself as a Mexican, hates "gringos," and rebels against being sent to the states for his higher education. Motley had planned to give the story of the Whitehorn family a further ironic twist by having Hal marry a dark-skinned Indian, but he ultimately softened the family's portrayal.

An American homosexual narrowly escapes being a genuine villain. Chester, unlike the sympathetically portrayed Owen of *Knock on Any Door,* seems cool and methodical in his seduction of boys between the ages of twelve and fourteen. He maintains that he does not really hurt the boys, that they grow up to marry and lead normal lives. However, Andrés, one of his boys, becomes a confirmed homosexual; and Chester is genuinely appalled at what he has done. When he confesses to Tom Van Pelt that he is unable to help himself, the reader's sympathy is stirred.

As these descriptions illustrate, Motley was creating more than an oversimplified scheme in which the American despoilers arrive in a paradise and corrupt it. The *norteamericanos* often act out of ignorance rather than malice, and the Mexicans themselves are not free of cupidity and selfishness. Only the overly sensitive or superficial reader could see the book as primarily anti-American, yet many reviewers did just that.

His sudden death before the publication of *Let Noon Be Fair* spared Motley the pain of an extremely adverse critical reaction, perhaps the worst of his career. Some reviewers, such as Robert H. Donahugh, seemed to assume that Motley had cynically attempted to grind out a best seller by emphasizing sex in a resort town. Donahugh summed up his assessment by predicting, rather inaccurately, that *Let Noon Be Fair* "will probably be popular, but the only significance it would have for libraries is to raise circulation statistics."[7] Even Jack Conroy, one of Motley's oldest literary friends, obviously thought the book disappointing, although he directed his criticism not at Motley but at the publisher, whom he considered responsible for Motley's writing the kind of book *Noon* turned out to be.

In a review for *Panorama,* a weekly supplement of the Chicago *Daily News,* Conroy recalled early plans for the book from his conversations with Motley and then asserted, "But authors, like actors, can be damagingly typecast. Motley, the hard-boiled, had to write something sensational and explosive in order to get published at all."[8] Conroy was, of course, only partially right. He mentioned the failure of "My House Is Your House" to find a publisher, a failure that was partly due to the lack of sensationalism in that book. However, *Let Noon Be Fair* was not the projected humorous novel Motley had discussed with his friend in 1961. From the start, the novel with the working title "Tourist Town" was to expose the unfavorable influence of American tourism in Mexico.

The New York *Times* gave the book not one but two unfavorable reviews. Charles Poore, who knew Motley's work, expressed disappointment with the latest novel in the daily *Times:* "Persons out for a holiday fling demand chances to fling, and that's the moral, I suppose, of 'Let Noon Be Fair.' Indeed, it tends to sound, in its stubborn emphasis on orgies, as though a cutoff date had been set for the methodical gee-whiz extravagances of the contemporary novel. Only creeping boredom can do that."[9] The *Times Book Review* carried a more thoughtful analysis by Alexander Coleman, who contrasted *Noon* with D. H. Lawrence's *The Plumed Serpent* and found Motley's novel weak as a picture of Mexican life. Coleman did not accuse the author of cheap sensationalism in his use of sexual material, but he considered Motley's analysis of the downfall of Las Casas to be "superficial and commonplace. The book has no real direction. New characters are introduced catalogue-fashion, with no depth or insight. The Americans are pallid and unconvincing, while the Mexicans shuffle through their roles — the corrupt *cacique,* the whiskey priest, the gay prostitute — without any penetration at all into the elusive character of Mexico. Motley has fallen into every trap the picturesque could offer."[10]

Jose Donoso, writing for *Saturday Review,* termed *Let Noon Be Fair* "an empty carcass of the panoramic novel." He felt that the novelist substituted quantity for psychological depth and precise style. He complained:

An exposé of corruption seems to be the author's intention. But his story is so linear and so relentless in its tracking of decay (epitomized by the talk, on the last page, of building a Hilton Hotel), that it leaves no place for irony. Without irony, Willard Motley's compassion looks more like sentimentality, and sentimentality is, in the end, lack of knowledge, of understanding, and of respect.... But by not exploring the complexities and paradoxes that both innocence and corruption entail ... Mr. Motley leaves us with the suspicion that he is really lamenting what even the cheapest tourist will bewail: the loss of local color in the place in the sun which *he* had discovered, and which has now become so expensive and so sadly "spoilt."[11]

No critic who really knew Motley's work could have made such a statement, nor does a careful reading of the book support the charge that Motley is simply exploiting the picturesqueness of small town Mexico.

Nelson Algren, who had panned *Let No Man Write My Epitaph,* wrote a curious piece for *Book Week* that is part elegy for Motley and part bittersweet review of his last book. Although he criticized Motley for using too many characters without developing them fully enough, Algren liked Motley's scathing criticism of the American middle class tourist, and he related it to the antibusiness tradition of Chicago novelists such as Dreiser, Anderson, and Wright. On the other hand, when he noted a tendency for the Americans to blend with one another, in contrast to the Mexican characters who seemed more real, Algren postulated, "This, I take it, is because the natives' lives are more real than are those of the touristas [*sic*]"; but Algren apparently felt that the technique was not successful. On the whole, he seemed to feel that Willard Motley's "last, saddest and most skillful book" was not a terribly good piece of work, and the general tone of the review is one of real or assumed pity for a writer whose work and personal life contained no "zest or joy."[12] One can only speculate whether part of Algren's review grew out of defensiveness toward a writer whom he may have considered a rival.

In spite of the bad critical reaction, *Let Noon Be Fair* sold well enough to encourage Dell to publish a paperback edition; but, since both editions were out of print by the early 1970s, Motley's attempt to explore new subjects and techniques could hardly be termed either a critical or a commercial success.

III   *Motley's Portrait of Mexico*

Much as he had moved in with the poor people of Chicago and then written of their strengths, their weaknesses, and their problems, Motley now observed the Mexican people and explored some of the difficulties they faced. In "My House Is Your House," he treats these problems in familiar essays; in *Let Noon Be Fair,* they emerge gradually from the novel. As a result, one of the major themes is the poverty of the Mexican people and the reasons for that poverty. While some readers apparently saw American exploitation as the only root cause of the economic suffering, Motley in fact presented a far more complex view. The poor people of Mexico can find no escape from their poverty because they are caught up in a lifestyle whose religious and secular pressures act to keep them poor.

Though at times Motley may stray too far toward sentimentality, he presents some touching pictures of the results of poverty: a good example is Ignacio. Coming from the same sort of background as his master Tizoc, Ignacio remains poor because, unlike Tizoc, he is honest. His wife bears him a child each year, but when some die during infancy, Ignacio rejoices — for children safe in heaven do not have to bear the cruelty of life. Ignacio lives without hope for himself or his children, an attitude that Americans undoubtedly found hard to understand. But he knows that he is a peasant and that nothing he can do will raise his wages or allow him to escape his station. When Tizoc, drunk and for once feeling generous, gives Ignacio a cash Christmas present, Ignacio takes his favorite son Margarito to Mexico City. Buying him a toy bus, he takes the boy to the park:

"Play," he told his son.
Margarito played with the bus there on the red tiles. He became engrossed. His back was to Ignacio and he was two benches down the tiles. That Ignacio would remember.
Ignacio, acting in the desperation of a desperate man, got up off the park bench. He squared his shoulders and walked away. He didn't look back.
. . . .
The smartest one must have a chance, he kept saying over and over to himself.[13]

Like the reformer he was, Motley was incapable of writing about the poverty of the Mexicans without speculating about the causes that underlay it. One of these, in his opinion, was the power of the Catholic church in Mexico and the uses to which that power was put. Sometimes the actual dogma of the church is at fault, as in the case of Ignacio and his ever-increasing family, for the official Catholic stand against birth control disregards the fact that poor families cannot possibly provide for as many children as they can produce. Thus, Father Campos hews to the teaching of the church (as he never does in regulating his own life) and refuses to permit

Cathy Mathews to teach family planning in the town library. Another side of the Mexican Catholic church that Motley, himself a Catholic, could not countenance was its hunger for the material possessions of its members. Before the feast day of the Virgin of the Sea, patroness of Las Casas, the *santa* or statue of the Virgin Mary is placed outside the church so that the people may kneel before it and contribute their pesos and centavos, money that might have fed their hungry children.

Besides objecting to inflexible doctrines of the church itself, Motley was strongly critical of the clergy's abuse of power. To the Mexican peasant, his parish priest's commands, even if occasioned by his cupidity or lust for power, are virtually indistinguishable from official dogma; and Motley emphasizes the corruption that this sort of power breeds. Thus, greedy Father Campos can demand that people who come to confess pay for their absolution as well as say a penance of prayers. Motley blamed the church authorities for permitting such abuses, as when he satirically points out that "nuns eat well, even the Little Sisters of the Poor" (346) in his description of Paz Beltran's fat friend from the convent.

Motley's reservations about the church are expressed through his characterization of Mario's father, the village freethinker. Although the women of his family are all devout Catholics, Señor Serrano rebels against the corruption within the church. On his deathbed, he refuses the last rites offered by Father Campos and asks him, " 'Are you not the man who rolled in the grass with María Camacho, the prostitute, the rich madam who clothes and feeds her son — your son? Do you not have a young son walking the streets of this village?' He pushed the prayer book away" (281). When he finally agrees to confess his sins and take communion, he does so only to quiet the grief of his wife.

Secular causes of the poverty also emerge, for Motley illustrates the prevalence of graft in the story of a new *presidente* who is appointed to govern Las Casas and its environs. Having perceived the possibilities that the town offers as a potential money-maker in the tourist trade, *el presidente* plans to expand the boundary lines of the town, buy the newly annexed land from the peon owners for a fraction of its value, and "develop" it by building a country club and a huge hotel. He bribes those capable of stopping his venture — Beltran and Tizoc — by offering them a share in it. The deal fails only because the official's greed is stronger than his instinct for self-preservation: he locks up the liquor distilled by the Indians of the hills. When a delegate from the distillers demands that he pay for their liquor, *el presidente* laughs at the peasant and replies that, since *caña* is made illegally, he has confiscated it; if the Indians persist in demanding payment, he will send soldiers to destroy their equipment. The Indian delegate seems humble, but

> The next morning ... two Indians sat on the curbstone in front of the *presidente's* house doing nothing but sharpening a machete and a long knife, occasionally testing the blades, first with thumbnail, then with a long, black strand of hair.
> The Indians sent word to the *presidente* that if he put foot on the street he would never cross it.
> . . . .
> The *presidente* took it for three days and then, with a guard of troops, he went to the airport and got on the plane and never came back again.
> Two rifle bullets whistled after the plane in send-off.   (57–58)

Like Carl Sandburg in *The People, Yes,* Motley has great faith in these little people who can act even without formal leadership when their basic dignity is threatened. Tizoc, the rich Indian, always seems more admirable than his rival Beltran, partly because he maintains his common touch. He prefers the beans and tortillas of his Indian heritage to the Armour turkey and other imported foods that his wife serves to guests.

In spite of great sympathy and understanding, Motley was sometimes puzzled by the Mexicans. Having faced racial prejudice himself in the United States, he wondered at the Mexican attitude toward skin color and facial configuration that indicate the presence of Indian blood. Although he told interviewers that he himself felt free from discrimination in Mexico, his novel reflects his observations about Mexico's own color line. Proud as he is of his Indian heritage, Tizoc has married a very white woman, whose Indian ancestry is apparent only in her prominent cheekbones. A person of "pure" Spanish ancestry takes an immense step down if he marries a *mestizo* or an Indian. Thus, when Paz Beltran renounces life by taking her final vows, her mother reflects hyperbolically that it would have been easier to accept her marriage to an Indian than this irrevocable act.

Motley was also bewildered by the Mexican attitude toward sex. The concept of *macho,* or rugged, bull-like masculinity, is exemplified by Tizoc, who is inordinately proud of his wife's pregnancy after both of them have attained middle age, and by Mario, who stands up to Tizoc, almost daring him to use the horsewhip he holds, after Yolanda confesses that Mario fathered the baby she is bearing. Although Motley, like the good Naturalist he is, faithfully presents Mexican men flaunting their *machismo* in *Let Noon Be Fair,* passages throughout "My House Is Your House" and his journal for the 1960s reveal that the author never truly understood the attitude.

A related sexual attitude prevalent in Mexico is the double standard that demands chastity of women but allows men unlimited freedom. In several ways Motley subtly exposes the hypocrisy of the double standard, as when Tizoc begins to keep an American mistress (or "to open a second front" as the practice is known in Mexico) and shows off by appearing in public with his flashy "gringa." The contrasts between his fat, peasant figure and the slimness of his hired consort, between his loud, vulgar laughter and the studied sophistication of his mistress, undercut the image Tizoc is trying to project. Similarly, María Camacho, while catering to strayed husbands, reminds them of their own hypocrisy when she demands that they show her a politeness that they would never practice toward their wives. Finally, Motley's sympathy toward the sheltered yet dominated women of the upper class is evident when Señora Beltran tells her husband that she is sending Paz to finishing school in France so that one of her daughters will be more than just a wife and will have an identity of her own.

In addition to puzzlement over racial and sexual attitudes, Motley found it difficult to understand the Catholics of Mexico. For example, he was shocked by their blasphemous jokes ridiculing the clergy, pious lay people, and even the saints and God himself. During his years in Mexico, the author collected these jokes, which he has Father Campos tell in *Let Noon Be Fair.* Motley also felt that some customs of the church verged on the pagan. The foremost example of an almost barbaric rite occurs when Paz takes her final vows, becoming a "bride of Christ." Paz takes a dowry to her order just as she might have taken it to a husband, and she wears a wedding dress and inherited jewelry just as she would have done at her wedding. However, the feeling that she is renouncing life rather than embracing it throws a macabre pall over the ceremony, and the relatives and friends who have come to the "wedding" leave it feeling depressed rather than happy.

Motley is much less ambivalent when he treats his major theme

— the deleterious effects of American domination of the Mexicans. An early indication of the "gringo" character comes when Motley sketches an unlovely American tourist, whose external ugliness mirrors her shallow and worthless character: "She wore a broad-brimmed straw hat with a farmyard of straw animals circling it. The hat had come from Acapulco. A bicycle tire tube of fat lay exposed between the bottom and top of her swimming suit. On her feet were sandals from Cuernavaca out of which, like teeth bared, highly red-polished toenails protruded, and on her fingers were large and heavy silver rings from Taxco" (8–9). Like many Americans in the novel, she has taken over certain articles of Mexican apparel and, by wearing them, she debases them. Nearby is José, El Indio, a poor man who makes his meager living selling Coca-Cola and beer. The dignity of José's person is ironically contrasted with "a T-shirt someone, possibly some gringo, had given him long ago on which was printed the world-recognized profile of Mickey Mouse" (9). In spite of the lady tourist's assertion that the people of Las Casas are "so unspoiled!" the handwriting is on the wall, and even El Indio, despite his illiteracy, can read it. What Motley does with clothing here capsulizes the process of Americanization: Americans take on certain facets of Mexican culture and cheapen them, and Mexicans assume many of the more vulgar traits of the Americans.

As their numbers increase, the gringos exert pressures that change the entire economic, moral, and cultural character of the town.

The Mexican government recognizes the dangers of foreign economic exploitation and attempts to curb it with various laws, such as the one that prohibits an alien from owning beach property; but the ingenuity of the developers is too great to be so easily circumvented, and Mexican "dummy" partners are brought into the foreign enterprises. The friendly local whorehouse is challenged by the more commercial establishment of Zimmer and Crowe, two entrepreneurs who eventually buy María's house. Foreign capital erects huge hotels that offer tourists impersonal, standardized convenience and luxury in place of the charming atmosphere of Julio Segovia's somewhat primitive Little Rose Hotel. Improvements include a major highway to accommodate tourists' cars and a pier, so that natives who unloaded ships for decades with dugouts are deprived of jobs. The cheap but slow method is simply not businesslike enough for the new economic rulers of Las Casas. One of the most pervasive and significant effects of the American invasion is that Spanish is treated as an inferior language while English becomes an absolute necessity for anyone connected with the tourist trade. Nearly every shop has a sign (usually in English) proclaiming that English is spoken therein. Little wonder, then, that young Mexicans either resent the foreign interlopers or are completely brainwashed into thinking their own culture worthless.

More dramatic is the sexual exploitation of the villagers. The brothers Tomás and Andrés, sons of a poor fisherman, illustrate the corrupting influences of the *norteamericanos* as they lose their integrity, each in his own way. Tomás, a handsome teenager, attracts the attention of Stella, a beautiful American who has slept with many Mexican men in her search for sexual excitement. She seduces Tomás, loses interest, and drops him. Some years later, when Tomás has a similar experience, he becomes dissatisfied with his poorly paid work as a hotel desk clerk and decides to profit from the appetites of the Americans. Quitting his job, he hangs out on the beach, where he attracts his first customer, a middle-aged man who pays him more than three months' salary for spending one night with him.

Andrés is one of Chester's young men who does not grow up to be a well-adjusted heterosexual. In spite of his feelings of guilt and shame, Andrés continues to see Chester even though the latter dislikes mature partners. Andrés becomes more overt in his homosexual behavior than Chester has ever been, for he sometimes wears makeup and makes it clear that he is a queen. Motley, who broadens the case as the American presence grows more dominant, depicts Andrés in a gay bar where straight tourists come to laugh at the inhabitants and where gay tourists come for pickups.

This moral disintegration affects even the most respectable society of the village. Doctor Ortega, once the only doctor in town, had previously refused to perform illegal operations. Now he feels the pressures of social changes in Las Casas: "Doctor Ortega took an occasional abortion case, even after Doctor Snyder was back from Europe. Then more. Occasionally he made out prescriptions for heroin and morphine for a few of the wealthy American residents, but only when he felt that they absolutely had to have it to carry on. In both instances he felt that he was morally right in these individual cases or he would not have done it. He was ashamed of all the money he was recently banking" (388).

Less insidious but far more obvious are the small but omnipresent external signs that the distinctive culture of the village is being replaced by something with far less dignity. Americans feel suspicion and contempt for traditional Mexican foods, and most are not bold enough to try them. Soon hot dogs and hamburgers predominate, and even the Mexican children begin to prefer them, reasoning that what the rich foreigners eat must be best. A nonconformist like his father, Mario starts a restaurant specifically to counter this movement. Furnished simply, it serves native dishes at low prices, although as a joke Mario hangs up a sign:

> American Curiosities:
> Hot Dogs
> Hamburgers (372)

On the whole, no reader can come away from the book without understanding some of the reasons why Mexico feels threatened by its proximity to the United States.

IV   *A Limited Success*

As Nelson Algren suggested somewhat backhandedly in his review of the book, *Let Noon Be Fair* does show signs that Motley was continuing to grow in his practice of the novelist's craft. Just as he had attempted to broaden his scope in *We Fished All Night,* he tried in his last novel to transcend some of the techniques and much of the subject matter that had made him famous in the 1940s. And despite its faults, *Let Noon Be Fair* is vastly superior to Motley's unsuccessful second novel. Rather than focus on a single powerful character as he had done in *Knock on Any Door,* Motley takes the town itself as his principle character and peoples it with a wide range of individuals, good and bad, sympathetic and unsympathetic, aristocrat and peon.

Although he had sometimes exhibited a tendency to dwell on or exaggerate the picturesque, a tendency evident since the *Hull-House Magazine* sketches and then in parts of *Let No Man Write My Epitaph,* Motley avoids this pitfall, even though the exotic atmosphere of Mexico would lend itself to such a treatment. The details of local color that he selects for inclusion in *Let Noon Be Fair* are carefully and precisely chosen for their effects, and he avoids the overly lengthy descriptive catalogues so characteristic of his earlier, more Naturalistic works. In fact, in this last novel, Motley seems to move farther than ever from the sort of doctrinaire Naturalism that characterizes his first work. In place of the unrelieved pessimistic determinism of *Knock on Any Door,* the reader finds the deterioration of Las Casas punctuated by numerous comic episodes, ranging from Tizoc's practical jokes to María's ironic invective, from Father Campos's collection of anti-Catholic jokes to farcical scenes such as a comic student revolt against governmental authority. Generally, except for a few lapses, the book is technically more mature than anything Motley had previously written.

Let Noon Be Fair shows intellectual growth as well as artistic growth. In earlier works, Motley had chosen convenient scapegoats to explain the failures of society — the law and the penal system in *Knock on Any Door,* war and political corruption in *We Fished All Night,* and narcotics traffic in *Let No Man Write My Epitaph.* However, in his last novel he seemed to be moving closer to the roots of many of America's social ills and of the ills of mankind in general. By exposing the widespread corruption that arises from overreliance on and preoccupation with material things, Motley lays bare many of the essential weaknesses in his native country and also in his adopted country. It is as if leaving his own city and his own country had given him the perspective to see basic causes rather than isolated symptoms. Those reviewers who saw the book as too critical of Americans were perhaps revealing their own biases and defensiveness more than any intrinsic weakness in the novel.

On the other hand, as Motley had feared, there are weaknesses in the book. Always frank in dealing with sex, Motley had allowed himself to be talked into using more explicit sexuality than he had thought necessary. In one early letter to Peter Israel, Motley worried that too much sex too early in the book would cause the reader to become bored with it (just as critic Charles Poore indicated he was bored).[14] Another weakness is the overuse of vignettes: some of the episodes involving Americans who appear only briefly could have been omitted without affecting the basic concept of the novel. The most serious fault is the absence of a well-defined and continuing conflict. Petty conflicts arise and subside throughout the book and the major conflicts between honesty and dishonesty and between tradition and garish change are present throughout, but they need reinforcement by one or more objective correlatives.

Nevertheless, the book's strengths so outweigh its weaknesses that it is difficult to understand the harsh reaction of reviewers.

Judgments may have been colored by the fact that some critics felt Motley was moving into an area where he had no business (the typecast theory of Jack Conroy) or by the fact that, as many reviewers unwittingly indicate, it is unpleasant for American readers to be chastised by black expatriate writers. Like his more famous contemporary Richard Wright, Motley seems to have irritated readers and critics when he began to compare his native country unfavorably with other countries. The liberal audience had learned by midcentury to tolerate or even to appreciate certain kinds of criticism from Afro-American writers, but perhaps it still considered them as specialists in domestic race relations and felt that they spoke about international issues only at their peril.

CHAPTER 6

Minor Works: The Final Years

BESIDES finishing *Let Noon Be Fair,* Motley spent the last years of his life writing his nonfiction book about Mexico and attempting to find a publisher for it. Several other projects included a short novel based on the history of his family, some stories, and short pieces of nonfiction. In addition, time and distance allowed him to reflect about trends in Afro-American literature and about critical responses to them; he often expressed distaste for some of the developments of the 1960s, most notably in a letter to *Time* magazine concerning James Baldwin.

I *"My House Is Your House"*

As early as 1953, Motley had been making notes and writing brief essays on his early impressions and feelings about life in Mexico. During the late 1950s, these fragments began to seem a viable basis for a book, and he set about the project of unifying them. Eventually he wrote considerable new material, producing a typescript of some five hundred pages; but from the beginning, "My House Is Your House" was a book that would be difficult to market because of publishers' taboos at that time. Although it is by no means a principal theme of the book, Motley's comparison of racial attitudes in Mexico with those in the United States inevitably resulted in frank statements about the color problem in America.

The chief occasion for such comparisons was the appearance in Mexico of various overbearing American tourists who ridiculed the natives and openly displayed contempt for them. Motley, who had thrown himself into the culture of Mexico as completely as he had earlier thrown himself into the milieu of the Maxwell Street and West Madison slums, had no more sympathy for such tourists than he had displayed for the sightseers who toured skid row Chicago

129

and made fun of the derelicts. But, to worried white publishers and agents who wanted to believe that America's racial problem had ended in 1954 with the Supreme Court's landmark decision about school integration, the book seemed to pick unnecessary quarrels at the slightest provocation.

In fact, Motley now seemed about to make a belated contribution to the protest movement that he had ignored when it was at its height. Even today some of the anecdotes seem contrived, as when Motley relates in great detail the story of how a black friend, Roland, had to pose as a chauffeur while driving to Mexico through the segregated South with three white companions, two of whom were women. Similarly, Motley's frequent allusions to prejudiced Texans seem to create an oversimplified stereotype, and his references to Federal Bureau of Investigation agents and informers, on the prowl for disloyal Americans who might let something slip while abroad, almost suggest paranoia at times.

On the other hand, most of the racial material in the book is an integral part of Motley's view of the two cultures and simply could not have been left out. As Motley told an *Ebony* interviewer in 1958, he did feel a freedom from prejudice in Mexico that he had never enjoyed in the United States.[1] One chapter in particular points out the extreme differences between Mexican and American attitudes, and it ranks with the best writing Motley ever published. In Chapter 31, "The States Again," Motley tells of a trip to Texas during which he and his aged mother, Mae Motley, were to renew their tourist cards. Mrs. Motley was to return to Motley's Mexican home directly, but the author was to make a trip to Chicago and New York. With them was Art O'Leary, one of Motley's oldest friends.

On a hot summer afternoon, the Motleys crossed from Nuevo Laredo to Laredo, Texas, and began searching for a hotel that would accept black guests. After taking them from hotel to hotel, their Mexican American cab driver finally rented rooms for them in a depressing flophouse over a tavern. Leaving their baggage, they set out on foot in the one hundred and three degree heat to find a restaurant. After being turned away from two, they found a greasy spoon that would accept two black people; but, by suppertime, this restaurant was closed and no other would serve them. Finally they bought Mrs. Motley a pint of ice cream, and Art, safe in his whiteness, went to a nearby restaurant and borrowed a spoon. Once his mother was in bed, Willard joined Art in the tavern downstairs for a beer. The proprietor, who also ran the hotel, told them that they would have to leave first thing in the morning because the driver had failed to tell him that two of his fares were "colored."

The next morning Willard consigned his mother to Art's care and boarded a train for the North. To the amusement of the black porters, he had purchased a first class ticket. Smiling at this innocent, who had reached his late forties without learning the facts of life, they showed him to the colored car. Willard consoled himself by spending most of the trip in the club car, to which his first class ticket admitted him, drinking beer and reflecting on his native land.

Meanwhile, Art O'Leary and Mae Motley were having more trouble than anticipated. After killing most of the day walking and sitting on park benches, they reported to the depot at five o'clock in the afternoon to catch the train. However, a storm had delayed it six hours, and the station was closing for the night. Once again Mrs. Motley had no place to go. They found a boarding house that proved to be so filthy that Mae Motley would not stay in it, then were directed by mistake to a brothel where, ironically, the madam welcomed them. Mae Motley elected to return to the filthy boarding house, where she and Art waited for the train on bedbug-free wooden chairs. At last, after two more delays which they sat out at the station, the train pulled in and delivered them from Laredo.

Motley, stopping over in Houston on his way to Chicago, had another bad experience with Texas hotels. When he and his white friend tried to find rooms in a white hotel, Willard was insulted; then, when they tried a black hotel, it refused to admit a white. They spent the night sleeping in chairs in the small apartment of a mutual friend. While such episodes are by no means typical of the entire book, his New York publishers and agents seemed to feel that this chapter and a few other sections like it outweighed the rest of the material. In a letter dated May 5, 1960, Mavis McIntosh, one of Motley's agents, suggested that Motley's sections on prejudice should be revised.[2] Her feeling for the attitudes of publishers was confirmed when the book was finally submitted, with the racial comments intact, to Robert Loomis, Motley's editor at Random House. Loomis expressed concern about what he felt was Motley's hatred for white Americans, and he eventually rejected the book, although not solely on those grounds.[3]

But there is much more to "My House Is Your House" than this comparison of racial attitudes. The entire manuscript reflects Motley's sincere desire to know the Mexican people — to learn their language, to eat their foods, to share their customs. His curiosity is not the idle interest of a tourist or the detached observation of a writer seeking new literary capital: it is a sort of tribute, a sign of the respect he felt for the people of Mexico.

The four sections of "My House" published in *Rogue* in 1964 and 1965 illustrate the range of the book's chapters. "A Kilo of Tortillas, a Güaje of Pulque" appears at first to be just another exotic food article of the type often carried by travel magazines. However, even this first *Rogue* piece is much less tourist-oriented and is more informative than the average travel article, for Motley shows the importance of *pulque* to the Mexican peasant and debunks stories that are told about the hard liquors of the country — *tequila, mescal,* and *caña.* Motley points out that the average tourist may sample these liquors, but the peasant, who cannot afford them, satisfies his thirst with the real beverage of Mexico — *pulque,* a beerlike drink. He takes the reader into the clublike atmosphere of the *pulqueria,* a shrine of *machismo:*

They are much like old-time saloons and even retain, in most cases, the swinging doors and the sawdust floor, though in the poorer neighborhoods the floor is lumpy, hard-packed dirt. Only *pulque* is sold there while men play dominos or pitch coins at a hole in a board. Women are not admitted but may buy *pulque* from a little window on the side. Often in slum neighborhoods you see men and women sitting together on the curb, drinking from *güajes* (gourds shaped somewhat like Mae West if she had no head and no legs...) or from milk bottles, mothers giving a bit to suckling babies, and little boys in their ever-fashionable shirt and no pants stealing from the bottle when their parents aren't looking.[4]

Motley points out the fascinating names of such *pulquerias*: 'My Illusions," "Memories of the Future," "My Office," "I'm Waiting For You Here at the Corner."

When he treats food, Motley does not cater to the tourist, but describes things he will never taste, as well as restaurant dishes. Some foods seem unappetizing to a North American; in addition to fried grasshoppers, there is the "*jumil* that is about as big as a bee, but flat. This is eaten by farmers and the poor and also, sometimes, by the extravagantly rich (for kicks). The black ones smell like bedbugs and are not eaten but the dark grey ones are eagerly sought after." Carried to work in cans or jars by farmhands, the live insects are dumped into warm *tacos*: "Sometimes an insect or two escapes, crawls over the eater's lips and is shoved back into the mouth."[5] Although Motley's tone is predominantly light, he does not let his reader forget that many of these foods, like black American "soul foods," have their origins in a terrible and crushing poverty.

More unusual is Motley's treatment of his experiences in Mexican whorehouses. The title "Give the Gentleman What He Wants" is a humorous dig at the expectations of *Rogue*'s audience, for the framework of Motley's observations about the brothel as a social institution south of the border is his effort to learn the language by paying for the time of a prostitute who sits with him and talks to him. As Motley observes, the Mexican whorehouse is far less furtive and more genteel than its equivalent in other countries, but his behavior was considered odd even in this context. Spotting a book on English in the hands of one prostitute, Motley befriended her and taught her English as she taught him Spanish; from time to time, he ordered drinks to keep the girl's madame happy. Motley treats his own role with humor, as he relates how he first thought that he was the girl's benefactor, that when she had learned English, she would leave the house and become an "honest woman." Moreover, he also exaggerates his feeling of foolishness when he learns that she is interested in English because so many Americans come to the house.

On the other hand, he points out the serious side of the girl's life as well, a sadness she feels because she cannot be part of a stable family. Motley accents the irony of the Catholic country's religious feelings: "The most improbable and amazing thing of all is this: each room has a sort of antechamber, a small room in front of the bedroom. Invariably, in this little room near the door that opens upon sex and sale, there is a little altar on which is displayed a statue or holy picture, generally of the Virgin of Guadalupe, with holy candles burning in front of it ... a little vigil light. *Watch over us.... Virgin of Guadalupe. In our weakness, our sins, our enterprises....*"[6] He also observes a symbolic fitness in the geography of Cuernavaca: "Ironically, or perhaps by a strange (though factual) relationship in society, the whorehouse, the cathedral and the police station are all within a block of each other."[7] This suggestion that the people of Mexico are imprisoned and bled by their government and by their church is explicit as well as implicit throughout "My House Is Your House," just as it is in *Let Noon Be Fair*.

The other *Rogue* pieces included a description of the Mexican celebration of Christmas, complete with the household image of the infant Jesus, and by an eerie coincidence, a chapter entitled "Death Leaves a Candle," printed some six months after death had claimed its author. This last article examines the customs connected with November 1 and 2, All Saints' Day and All Souls' Day, when families visit the cemeteries and honor their dead. Motley, who found the celebration curiously pagan, was at first horrified: "I had looked with astonishment and repulsion into the bakery window. There, staring out at me, row after row, were little white skulls made of candy. Tiny, grinning, repulsive things, their eyes bright tinsel-red, green, blue, staring as in a nightmare. Their mouths, leering and lipless, the bare white teeth set forward — a grim death's head. And made of candy, for children."[8] But as he talked to his Mexican friends, Motley came to understand their apparently morbid preoccupation with death. In a country with high infant mortality, where health care for the very poor may be almost nonexistent, death had to be accepted. The inevitability of death, combined with the religious faith of the Mexican peasant, kept death from being hidden away as it is in American society. In the end, Motley acknowledged the wisdom of the Mexican attitude.

But the articles published in *Rogue* are only a very small part of a multifaceted study of Mexican life and culture. In unpublished chapters of the book, Motley discussed Mexican music and religion, the concept of *macho,* racial relations, and the poverty of the common people. While he is frequently complimentary toward the Mexicans themselves, the book is by no means a paean of unqualified praise for the country as a whole. For example, the Mexican man seemed to Motley to draw on the worst elements of feudal culture. Women were expected to be virtuous, while men were actively encouraged to behave like tomcats. Wealthy men kept their mistresses in high style, while the lower classes visited brothels or engaged in affairs. And, accustomed as he was to the rougher side of life, Motley found the Mexican custom of carrying pistols everywhere — or, if one was wealthy, hiring armed bodyguards, or *pistoleros* — to be a rather hollow assertion of virility.

The poverty that he observed disturbed Motley, for it was a more severe form of want than he had ever seen before, even in the Maxwell Street neighborhood of his early career. Children began to work or to steal as young as eight years of age, and beggars were found everywhere but in the smallest villages where poverty was nearly uniform. Men with nothing to offer but their strength turned themselves into beasts of burden, or *cargadores,* and spent their whole lives carrying huge heavy loads of other people's goods in order to eke out a living. The Catholic church, in which Motley himself had been brought up, did little to aid the common people; in fact, it even drained away some of their meager funds by encouraging them to donate far more than they could afford to its already bulging treasuries.

The lower levels of government, although purged repeatedly by revolution, continued to be marked by *la mordida,* or "the bite," whose rules decreed that any civil servants who could discover a method were entitled to bleed the people with whom they came in contact. Thus, border guards could be expected to find some irregularity in the luggage or papers of those who passed through their posts; local police allowed thieves' markets to operate under their very eyes; a minor traffic accident might turn into a nightmare if the driver did not respond to "the bite." Although Motley knew about the crooked politics and the payoffs in his native Chicago, he still found the extent of graft in Mexico incredible.

While he had praise for the absence of prejudice against blacks in Mexico, Motley noted that there were some strange quirks in the attitude toward Indians and those of mixed ancestry. Although many people with light skin might boast of their Indian blood and point to the presidency of Benito Juarez with pride, the pure Indian frequently occupied the bottom rungs of the economic and social ladders. Motley learned that the mustache worn by every boy or man old enough to grow one was an assertion of Spanish ancestry, for the pure Indian did not normally produce much facial hair. However, an important difference between racial attitudes in the two countries may be traced to the fact that, while Americans considered anyone with demonstrable Negro blood to be black, Mexicans considered anyone with some Spanish blood to be *mestizo* and therefore socially acceptable even though Indians were not.

Perhaps the greatest marks of Motley's attachment to Mexico are the completely personal chapters in which he tells the stories of two poor and fatherless Mexican boys whom he took in. Raul had been making his own way in the streets before meeting Motley, while Sergio had been cared for and educated as well as the slight means of his mother had permitted, but both needed the stability and warmth that the Motley household extended to them. Motley's love for the two boys emerges from the pages of the book as a microcosmic model of his affection for the Mexican people.

II   *"Remember Me to Mama"*

As early as 1947, Motley had indicated in a letter to his Appleton editor Ted Purdy that he hoped some day to write a novel based on the history of his own family; it was to cover three generations and emphasize the life of a character that would be modeled after his mother. Now, after completing "My House Is Your House" and before starting serious work on the novel tentatively entitled "Tourist Town," he wrote a short novel called "Remember Me to Mama." Feeling that the work invades their privacy, the Motley family has suppressed it; and the manuscript is not to be found in either of the major collections of Motley's papers. Motley himself apparently misjudged the sensitivity of his family, since he submitted the work to several publishers.

Although this family novel is quite short — the completed manuscript comes to only one hundred twenty-five pages of typescript — it took Motley a surprisingly long time to finish it. On July 22, 1960, he wrote his literary agent Elizabeth McKee that he intended to write what he called a "psychological mystery" before he went on to "Tourist Town." Although he seems to have done little actual work up to this point, he had arrived at the tentative title.[9] By August 2, he was into the writing of the novel, but it was a year and a half before he sent it to the McIntosh-McKee agency. "Remember Me to Mama" arrived at his agents' office on February 9, 1962, and on February 13 Elizabeth McKee wrote to Motley about the new book. She felt that the work was not up to Motley's usual standards, but she planned to send it to McGraw-Hill anyway, since that firm had expressed interest in seeing the manuscript. In one of the fastest evaluations ever accorded a submission, McGraw-Hill immediately rejected the work; and, by February 27, just a little over three weeks from the time the manuscript had reached her office, Elizabeth McKee was advising Motley that the work would probably never be published since "several" houses had rejected it by this time.[10] Yet Motley continued to believe in the book and to defend it in letters to his agent.[11]

Why was the manuscript rejected so summarily? The book may have been appallingly bad, or perhaps something about it caused the agents to react unfavorably and to convey their own negative reactions — deliberately or accidentally — to the publishers. Whatever Motley may have thought, he accepted the word of Elizabeth

McKee and shelved the book after the initial attempt to find a publisher failed.

In the absence of a manuscript, not much can be said about "Remember Me to Mama." Motley had told Ted Purdy in 1947 that he hoped someday to write a book "about Negroes, not as such, but as Negroes integrating themselves into the life of a big city (Chicago) or cracking up under the social and economic pressures."[12] He then sketched a plot line that would take the protagonist, a black Catholic woman born near New Orleans, to Chicago, where she bears two children. The novel would have continued with the life story of the main character and her two children, based on Motley's older brother and sister, and finally with the lives of their children. Since it would have been difficult to develop a plot covering so long a period of time in a typescript of only one hundred twenty-five pages, it seems unlikely that "Remember Me to Mama" was based on this plan.

In the same long letter to Purdy, however, Motley had sketched another plot idea that dealt with a family he did not identify as his own. This story was to have been about a boy who discovers that his outwardly respectable family has been torn by a scandal before his birth. More complex than anything Motley had written to that point, the story of the scandal was to be revealed from several points of view, with the boy left to determine the truth of the several accounts.[13] This story, more than that of the three generations, would seem to merit the "psychological mystery" description used by Motley in his first letter about the novel. It is to be hoped that the family will eventually follow the author's own wishes and release the manuscript so that scholars may judge the work on its literary merits.

III *Final Minor Projects*

In addition to the two books about Mexico and "Remember Me to Mama," several minor projects engaged Motley during the 1960s. Never very successful in placing his short fiction, the author was pleasantly surprised in June 1961 to receive a letter from Herbert Hill, a long-time official of the National Association for the Advancement of Colored People, asking him to contribute to an anthology that Hill was editing. "The Almost White Boy," written some twenty years before, had never been published; and Motley contributed that to Hill's anthology, published in 1963 as

Soon, One Morning: New Writing by American Negroes.[14] The
opportunity to publish a story that had been all but forgotten for
years set Motley to thinking about other early works that might
now be marketable, and he sent several short manuscripts to the
McIntosh-McKee agency, including one very short satirical piece
that he had written only recently.

Not a good story, "The Funnies: A Semi-Fictional Documenta-
tion of Our Times" is of interest because it expressed the growing
pessimism that Motley was feeling about life in general during his
last years. The framework of the story is similar to that used by
Ernest Hemingway in "The Gambler, the Nun and the Radio": a
critically ill man, expecting to die, lies in a hospital room where his
physical inactivity forces him to reflect on life. Trying to divert
himself from his own impending death, the man reads *Time* and
Newsweek magazines from cover to cover. Struck by the bizarre
ironies of a world gone mad, he begins to find the tragic stories
funny, and he laughs uproariously at the accounts of famine, pesti-
lence, and threats of nuclear war. Since the story, depending
heavily on actual news accounts paraphrased from the magazines,
does not succeed, the agents were never able to interest a publisher.

An idea from the past that Motley resurrected during the early
1960s was for a book of pictures and narration that he intended to
call "Sunday Afternoon, Skid Row, U.S.A." Inspired by his own
photographic essays during his days on the Writers' Project and by
his work with the *Look* photographers after the publication of
Knock on Any Door, this project would have teamed Motley with a
professional photographer. The two would have worked in Chicago
or some other large American city and would have contrasted
activities in a typical middle class neighborhood on a Sunday with
those on Skid Row; that is, scenes of "Church, washing the family
car in front of the family house, Sunday dinner, the kids going off
to the show" would have been juxtaposed with the scenes of
poverty typical in the lower class areas of the city, where Sunday
made little difference.[15] Unlike some of his later schemes, the book
sounds promising; but Motley was unable to find an interested
publisher.

Motley even thought of using his Writers' Project experience as a
writer of radio plays to break into the new medium of television. In
1962 he went so far as to write a script based on a part of *Let No
Man Write My Epitaph* and to send it to Elizabeth McKee, who
warned him that producing the television play would have violated

Motley's copyright agreements with Random House and with Hollywood. In the same vein, Motley toyed with the idea of a new screen version of *Knock on Any Door,* this one with a narrative more closely in line with his own conception of how the story should have been treated; but nothing came of this plan either.

IV   *Some Thoughts on Color*

Although his subject matter has usually differed markedly from that of other black writers, Motley was on good terms with several of his black contemporaries. In the fall of 1959 when Langston Hughes wrote Motley asking for the donation of an autographed book for a collection to be sent to Ghana, Motley replied by offering an autographed copy of his most recent novel, *Let No Man Write My Epitaph.* A brief correspondence ensued, and Hughes visited Motley briefly during a trip to Mexico. Hughes later classified Motley among "the noted names in American Negro writing" — along with Richard Wright, Ralph Ellison, and James Baldwin — in an editor's note to his anthology *Best Short Stories by Negro Writers* (1967), which reprinted "The Almost White Boy." [16]

Ann Petry, whose subject matter in *The Street* (1946) coincided with Motley's and who had also tried her hand at writing "raceless" fiction, greeted the publication of *Epitaph* with a letter of praise for Motley's latest book. She and Motley continued to exchange letters from time to time during the 1960s. [17] Frank London Brown, younger than Motley by some eighteen years, seems to have admired the older writer although he did not depend on him for direct advice about writing. Like Motley, Brown had been reared in Chicago, and he used the city as the setting of his first novel, *Trumbull Park* (1959). Their ideas about the treatment of the black struggle in their fiction differed, but Brown and Motley nevertheless seem to have had considerable respect for each other as novelists. [18]

On the other hand, Motley was irritated by James Baldwin. In 1961, after receiving a copy of Baldwin's *Nobody Knows My Name,* Motley told a relative that he resented what he deemed Baldwin's exploitation of his own blackness. [19] Later, when Baldwin made the cover of *Time* in 1963 and the magazine carried a story laced with quotations from interviews with Baldwin and from his speeches and works, Motley felt compelled to make a public statement. Among other things, *Time's* acerbic writer highlighted Bald-

win's disenchantment with white liberals and his destruction of the
myth that the North is a land of opportunity for black Americans.
Motley countered with a lengthy letter to the editor, only part of
which was printed. Calling Baldwin a "professional Negro," Motley told of several personal experiences that refuted Baldwin's
alleged assumption that all whites are united in their ill treatment of
blacks. He closed by saying,

> If I understand correctly, Mr. Baldwin does not like liberals. Well, I
> have news for him. There are thousands of radicals, liberals and just plain,
> ordinary white people in the United States who are people of good heart
> and have none of these prejudices he has taken his stake of land out in.
> Finally, the next time I go to Chicago, I must go by way of Birmingham,
> or wherever else there is trouble, for I feel it is time for every man, woman
> and child of good will to stand up and be counted.[20]

Partially because *Time* had not printed his entire letter and partially because the whole incident had started him thinking about his
youth and experiences relating to race, Motley was not willing to
drop the matter after writing his letter. Hoke Norris, the book editor of the Chicago *Sun-Times* who had occasionally bought reviews
from Motley, encouraged Motley to expand his ideas on the subject
of race into a full length article and to send it to the *Sun-Times*. In
late July, Motley sent Norris an essay called "Some Thoughts on
Color." After a few editorial cuts, the article appeared under the
rather inappropriate headline "Let No Man / Write Epitaph / Of
Hate For / His Chicago" in the Sunday *Sun-Times* of August 11,
1963. An editor's note related the article to Baldwin's *Time* interview and to Motley's response to it.[21]
Motley began by identifying himself not with a racial minority
but with the mass of mankind:

> A Negro, an American, but long before that and certainly forever after,
> just one of almost 3 billion people on this small, unhappy planet, I feel less
> like a Negro, an American, than I do like just one of the 3 billion and that
> where wrong is, there I should be in heart and at home: it is hard to iden-
> tify with a race — but only against an injustice.
> I never think of color until the subject is forced upon me: never think of
> the man sitting across from me — he's white! He's a Negro just like me![22]

He acknowledged that, in spite of his own feelings and experiences,
there is an inevitable problem in the United States: "That every

person in the United States is scarred by the Negro-white thing at birth, even those of good will, is indisputable. It is our national disease, some carriers, others victims, but all scarred; and, as yet, no scientist or doctor has, under his test tube and microscope, come up with a vaccine."[23] In his own case, Motley says, he first became aware of racial prejudice when an aunt who was visiting his family asked his mother how she could stand to live in a white neighborhood. On the other hand, during the race riots of 1919, these same white neighbors had helped to protect the Motley family from rampaging whites who might have harmed them for "block-busting."

Motley felt that his own experience in school suggested that he was actually favored because he was a member of a minority. He tells of a teacher in grammar school who befriended him and who told the rest of the class when he was absent that Willard "would amount to something some day." Older people in his own neighborhood seemed to accept Willard and his parents even though, in his hearing, they often insulted other minority groups — the "dagos," the "polacks," and the "greasers" — and on one occasion antiblack sentiment surfaced but was not directed at the Motleys.

The article generally develops, with a number of subjective examples, Motley's lifelong belief that "people are just people" and that people have to be judged as individuals and not lumped in with a larger class. He closes with an exhortation aimed at those who think and write as Baldwin does: "This 'hate the white man' is pretty childish stuff. There are too many white men of good will in this battle with him — this new white 'minority group' (and not so minor as some people think, nor is it so new)."[24]

Several things are noteworthy about this epistle. First, the tone is almost exactly that of the unfavorable review Motley had given Chester Himes' *Lonely Crusade* some fifteen years earlier. Unlike many black writers, Motley had not changed his essential position on racial relations over those years, in spite of the failure of the integration movement. True, he had begun to write of specific color problems in *Let No Man Write My Epitaph* and in his unpublished manuscript of "My House Is Your House," and he had given interviews that admitted that one factor in his move to Mexico had been the relative freedom from racial prejudice there.[25] But he still felt that the racial problems of the United States could best be solved by a partnership of the people of good will in both races. A second point of interest is that Motley relates racial prejudice to ethnic prejudice; to scorn a man because he comes from south of the Mexican border is just as ridiculous as to "jim-crow" him because he is black — a fact not stressed by many racial spokesmen. Finally, Motley's opening statement about being a citizen of the whole world suggests that, like his more famous contemporary Richard Wright, he had been led by his expatriation to think in international terms rather than to generalize solely on the basis of specific problems of the black American ghetto.

The article reinforces the impression created by his two books about Mexico — that Motley was evolving into a different type of writer, or at least into another type of thinker, than he had been in the 1940s and the 1950s. He was beginning to look for root causes for man's misery instead of merely offering specific examples of that misery. Yet the compassion and human sympathy that had first motivated him during the writing of *Knock on Any Door* remained a constant factor in his work.

V *Death Leaves a Candle*

On March 4, 1965, all projects came to an end. After four days in a Mexico City clinic, Motley died of gangrene, slipping away quietly during a lengthy coma. Little information is available about his last days. His final diary entry, dated February 19, 1965, merely notes the shipment of pages 1014 through 1129 of the "Tourist Town" manuscript to Putnam's. There is no indication that he had been injured or ill. His adopted son Sergio, in an epitaph that curiously echoed Motley's old nickname "the little iron man," remarked that "Willard always prided himself on not ever being sick and said he didn't need doctors. He let this illness go too long before getting proper medical attention."[26] Motley was buried in the cemetery at Cuernavaca, one of his favorite cities in Mexico.

CHAPTER 7

An Appraisal of Motley's Career

D URING his lifetime, Willard Motley was regarded more as a
minor celebrity than as a man of letters. To aspiring authors,
he was one man who had made it, who had learned the secret of
selling what he had written not only to the prestigious publishers of
hard cover books, but to the paperback reprint houses and to that
most lucrative market of all, Hollywood. To the black community
of his time, he was not just a success but a black man who had overcome the very special problems that race adds to the obstacles faced
by all writers. It made no difference that he chose not to write primarily about blacks; he was still one of their own, and they
respected him as they did Frank Yerby — for his success, if not for
his writing itself. To a few enthusiastic reviewers, he seemed to be a
major new talent when his first novel appeared, and when he failed
to become a giant, the newspaper reviewers were as ready to
condemn him as they had been to lionize him. Perhaps only a hand-
ful of his closest friends knew how devoted Willard Motley was to
his writing — how seriously he took both the literary techniques
and the social messages with which he was dealing. Looking back
on his career, however, one may now see the man and his work
more clearly than was possible during his life.

I A Latter-Day Naturalist

It was an unfortunate accident that Motley's favored subject
matter and his most effective style belonged to an earlier age. Had
he been born thirty or even ten years earlier, he would not have
seemed such an anachronism. As his career developed, however,
many of his contemporaries benefited from the various experiments of James Joyce, William Faulkner, John Dos Passos, and
Ernest Hemingway to produce works that eclipsed the Naturalistic

novels of the preceding generation. The type of novel that collected a huge body of evidence, that multiplied similar incidents and amassed detail in order to create its effect, was abandoned by most serious novelists of Motley's generation in favor of works that utilized more impressionistic and selective techniques. The characteristic attitudes and style of Naturalism were taken over by the hack writers who exaggerated and prostituted the explicit violence and the sex that had been a necessary part of novels by authors such as Frank Norris and Theodore Dreiser. Of Motley's contemporaries, perhaps only James T. Farrell and John O'Hara, whose own critical reputation is hardly secure, successfully labored on as practicing Naturalists of the old school. For a young writer beginning his career in the 1940s, to write Naturalistic novels was to relegate oneself to second class status among American novelists.

But the best of Motley's novels, *Knock on Any Door,* belongs as firmly in the older tradition as do Crane's *Maggie: A Girl of the Streets,* Norris's *McTeague,* Dreiser's *An American Tragedy,* Farrell's *Studs Lonigan,* or Wright's *Native Son.* Motley was not enough of an intellectual to devise a new voice for himself, nor was he unprincipled and imitative enough to ape the techniques developed by others. Finally, he lacked the stubborn tenacity that has enabled James T. Farrell to transcend similar limitations and produce a body of fiction that will probably earn him a reputation as a writer of minor American classics. Instead, after the publication of his first novel, Motley experimented uneasily with alien techniques that never quite suited his material and expressed himself in a way that was never again as heartfelt as the voice he had found in *Knock on Any Door.*

Publishers had their part in Motley's failure to achieve another success as great as his first. Always in need of money and an agreeable man by nature, Motley was ill equipped to resist the demands that his editors imposed. Had he been given a freer hand, he would have had a better chance to find his own way, to determine whether he would continue his attempt to reawaken a dying mode or alter his own work so that it would better fit the times.

The strongest elements in Motley's fiction all stem from the Naturalistic tradition, and the weaknesses appear when he attempts to force his material into more fashionable modes. No American writer really knew the lower depths of the American city so well as Motley, and early Naturalists such as Stephen Crane and Frank Norris had lacked the intense sympathy that truly close association with their characters' prototypes would have produced. Theodore Dreiser, though he emerged from the proletarian class, never probed as deeply into the skid rows of American cities as Motley was to do; even George Hurstwood's New York is a far more gentle place than Nick Romano's Chicago. Farrell, in spite of the erroneous impression created by critics who oversimplify his work, is basically a novelist of the middle class, not the lower class. And, while Motley is a lesser artist than Richard Wright, their purposes differ; for, aside from a few memorable details about the kitchenette apartments of the South Side, *Native Son* tells less of real life in a big city than it does of the internal torment of its protagonist. In his own niche of American literature, Motley produced at least one book that should be read by any student of Naturalism in America.

II *Critical Assessments*

Perhaps because the early praise accorded *Knock on Any Door* was excessive, Motley's reputation with the critics has suffered since the 1950s. In most of the literary histories that treat the categories of fiction into which his work fits, Motley is acknowledged only briefly and sometimes his work is disparaged. For example, Robert A. Bone in *The Negro Novel in America* (1958), describes the style of *Knock on Any Door* as "journalistic" and as "deadpan, pulled-punch, pseudo-Hemingway" and suggests that the novel lacked originality:

The truth is that in its main outlines [the novel] leans so heavily on *Native Son* as to border on plagiarism. Nick Romano, like Bigger Thomas, is a bad "dago" — as bad as Motley can make him, in order to intensify the general guilt. Like Bigger, he commits a symbolic murder which gives his life meaning ("This is what I was born to do"). The chase, the trial, the speech of Nick's lawyer ("I accuse society") is simply *Native Son* stripped of racial implications. The difference is that where Wright's treatment is condensed and selective, Motley's is detailed and exhaustive. In effect, Motley has borrowed terse symbolic episodes from *Native Son* and inflated them to naturalistic proportions.[1]

Bone supports his opinion of *Knock on Any Door* by a brief reference to *We Fished All Night,* which he contends will "amply demonstrate the limitations of [Motley's] talent."[2] Whatever the critic might think of Motley's style, a careful reading of both *Native Son* and *Knock on Any Door* disproves the "plagiarism" charge against Motley. If *Knock on Any Door* is plagiarized from *Native Son,* then the latter may be said to be plagiarized from

Dreiser's *An American Tragedy*. Like Clyde Griffiths, both Bigger Thomas and Nick Romano kill and are caught, tried, and executed. All three novels contradict a Horatio Alger type of assumption about man's ability to rise in American society. All three authors, having come from relatively humble origins, are moved to convey in their fiction the fate of the man who challenges this supposedly mobile society. Nick's plight is economic rather than racial, and his crime has nothing to do with sexual stereotypes as Bigger's does. Finally, the basic idea of *Knock on Any Door* was completely conceived by the time *Native Son* appeared in 1940.

Unlike Bone, many critics slight Motley more by what they do not say than by specific criticism. Chester Eisinger, in *Fiction of the Forties* (1963), devotes little space to Motley and concludes that he is not very important because he works in the outdated mode of Naturalism. Walter Rideout (*The Radical Novel in America*, 1956) discusses *Knock on Any Door* and *We Fished All Night* only briefly. Frederick J. Hoffman (*The Modern Novel in America*, 1951) devotes a few pages to a comparison of *Knock on Any Door* with Nelson Algren's *The Man With the Golden Arm*, but he accords neither the treatment in depth that he gives to novels that he considers truly significant.

On the other hand, Blanche Gelfant, in *The American City Novel* (1954) presents a more fairly balanced discussion of *Knock on Any Door*. She considers it comparable in many ways to Dreiser's *An American Tragedy* in that both novels attack social conditions as the true cause of criminal acts, both direct attention to the economic inequality that still prevails in America, and both stress the importance of environment. She feels, however, that Motley's novel does not achieve the complexity of *An American Tragedy*: "In order to stress the sociological thesis, [*Knock on Any Door*] has reduced character, situation, and setting to skeletal essentials. Thus, Nick is a stereotype of the juvenile driven to delinquency through bad influence. He lacks the individuality that Clyde had by virtue of his peculiar romantic and sensuous temperament...."[3] Although she feels that Motley's secondary characters tend to fall into stereotypes and that the symbolism is heavy handed, Professor Gelfant praises his handling of the novel's setting, his descending into the real lower depths of the American city, his documenting the dangers and violence of the big city underworld.

One critic of the early 1960s moved against the mainstream by praising Motley even before the resurgence of interest in black writers that was to mark the last half of the decade. In "James Baldwin and Two Footnotes," Harvey Breit discusses Motley in company with Baldwin and Ralph Ellison, a juxtaposition that some earlier critics would have considered audacious. Breit explains, however, that "a brief if muted tribute to Willard Motley is in order. He has written at least one novel that rises far above even the excellent naturalistic fiction of our generation. In his first novel . . . Motley tried to write a color-blind story and succeeded admirably. His impoverished, oppressed, harrassed and fleeing people were any people; for the purposes of his fiction they were white. It was, in effect, a distinct coup."[4] Emphasizing Motley's wish to be read as a writer "of no color or of all color, and not, one must rush to add, because of shame, humiliation or fear," Breit relates that E. M. Forster had asked him incredulously if Motley were really black. Besides Motley's ability to get inside the minds of his white characters, Breit also praises his compassion, sensitivity, and love — qualities that inform his fiction with something more than the standard tenets of Naturalism.

Nor was Breit the only critic of the 1960s to return to Motley. John F. Bayliss closes a 1969 essay on Motley's two Romano family novels by saying, "Motley deserves more critical space than he has been afforded. There is a minor Baldwin industry, but almost complete silence for Motley. As a Negro writer, his great achievement was to successfully project himself into the white mentality, and the two books reviewed here are worthy analyses of white humanity."[5] Some critics in the 1970s followed Bayliss's advice. The magazine that Bayliss edited, *Negro American Literature Forum,* featured a Willard Motley issue in 1972 and has since published several other articles on Motley's work; two prestigious general literary journals, *Proof* and *Resources for American Literary Study,* printed articles based on Motley's unpublished papers; and Motley's diaries from 1926 to 1943 were edited for publication.

Finally, while only *Knock on Any Door* and *Let No Man Write My Epitaph* were still in print at the beginning of the 1970s (the former only in its paperback edition), *We Fished All Night* was one of fifty books of poetry and fiction added to the 1974 list of reprints published by AMS Press, a pioneer in the reprinting of scarce materials in the field of black literature. After a period of being ignored or dismissed by the critics, Motley's work has seemingly demanded a revaluation.

III   *Motley's Place in Black Literature*

Considering the present flourishing state of Afro-American literature, Motley's preoccupation with white protagonists and with general social problems may seem to border on the pathological, perhaps to hint at what Robert Bone has called "his own inner conflict."[6] In the 1940s and 1950s, however, such a choice seemed a logical and viable alternative to writing about black characters and problems. Motley was by no means alone in writing nonblack books; in fact, Bone himself recognizes a category of "assimilationist" or "raceless" novels in his own literary history, and has summed up the rationale behind the movement: "What prompted this development was an understandable but unsophisticated desire for an 'integrated' art. Reasoning by simple analogy, the assimilationists argued that Negroes were at last breaking out of their ghettoes and moving toward full participation in every phase of American life. Why not art? Let the Negro novelist demonstrate his cosmopolitanism by writing of the dominant majority."[7] Nor was Bone the first to perceive this trend.

In a 1950 essay in which Charles I. Glicksberg protested what he called "The Alienation of Negro Literature," he asserted that critics in the past had been guilty of a "refined form of cultural segregation." He explained: "Negro writers are praised and encouraged for possessing talent that is authentically 'Negroid.' They are not *American* writers. They are Negroes, and that makes all the difference. Only those elements of their work which differentiate it *racially* from 'white' art are praised and encouraged, and since the whites for the most part control the aesthetic norms of appreciation as well as the channels of public recognition, they have helped to lay the foundation of what has been called 'Negro literature.' "[8] Glicksberg came to the conclusion that the black writer would attain major status only when he treated "all of life, all that is distinctly human" in his work.[9]

In another 1950 essay, Thomas D. Jarrett, like Glicksberg, concluded that the days of a distinct "Negro literature" were coming to an end. He suggested that if black writers were to attain truly mature art, they must move away from the racial protest that had earlier marked their writings: "there must be a growing social consciousness and a universality in the treatment of themes; and, concomitantly, there must be a higher regard for literary values if works that are meaningful and vital and of the first order are to be produced."[10]

Since Jarrett held these views, it is not surprising that he felt that *Knock on Any Door* had achieved the sort of universality for which he was pleading because Motley had written about a problem that could affect any racial or ethnic group that found itself in the grip of similar economic hardships. Although Jarrett mentioned other young black writers whom he considered promising, he singled Motley out for more extensive comment and praised his characters and his methods of conveying his social beliefs: "by means of analogy and artful pictorialization he sets forth his naturalistic social philosophy and expresses his indictment of society. Through well-chosen symbols ... he makes his main character a tragic exemplum of what can happen to an individual through society's neglect and active participation."[11]

While the critical and artistic pendulum has since moved in the opposite direction, it is important to recognize that, during the period of Motley's greatest artistic activity, critical essays in black periodicals were advancing this point of view.[12] Parallel with the critical movement toward nonracial or universal themes in the late 1940s and early 1950s, there was a distinct movement among Motley's fellow black novelists to produce a different type of novel. In the same year that *Knock on Any Door* appeared, Ann Petry, who had previously published a protest novel (*The Street,* 1946), turned to the life of a small New England town with *Country Place,* in which all the principal characters are white. Over the next few years, a number of other Afro-American novelists were to follow the example of Motley and Petry. In 1948 Zora Neale Hurston, who had published two novels about the black rural South during the 1930s, treated the life of the white South in *Seraph on the Suwanee.* Similarly, William Gardner Smith in 1950 employed predominantly white characters in his second novel, *Anger at Innocence.*

Some might object that Petry, Hurston, and Smith do not belong to the mainstream of the Afro-American tradition any more than Motley does; however, during the 1950s several writers who were undeniably from that tradition also published novels dealing with whites. The most famous of these authors was, of course, Richard Wright, whose *Savage Holiday* (1954) explored the psychological roots that influence an ultrarespectable retired insurance executive to cause the accidental death of a small boy and subsequently to murder the boy's mother. Although this novel was rather poorly received in the United States — it was never published in a hard

bound edition, but appeared as an Avon paperback original —
Wright himself never considered it a potboiler, and it was taken
more seriously in France, where it was published as *Le Dieu de
Mascarade.*[13] Similarly, both Chester Himes and James Baldwin
published "white" novels in the 1950s. Himes finally came to grips
with his prison experience, which had hitherto been reflected only
in short works, with the publication of *Cast the First Stone* (1952).
While black characters do appear in the prison novel, the protagonist is white, and the focus is primarily on white characters. *Gio-
vanni's Room* (1956), Baldwin's second novel, treated the problems
of white homosexuals living in Europe.

The difference between Motley's career and those of the other
writers mentioned is obvious, however. Each of the above authors
began his or her career by writing at least one work in which the
black cultural background was predominant before publishing a
"raceless" novel as an apparent experiment. Except for Zora Neale
Hurston, who never wrote another novel after *Seraph on the
Suwanee,* all returned to black life in their later fiction. Motley,
although he used black characters in important roles in *Let No Man
Write My Epitaph,* was never to publish a novel about purely black
life.

On the other hand, Motley's published and unpublished writing
and his correspondence seem to contradict Bone's suggestion that
Motley's failure to use the black experience more fully indicates
some deep antipathy toward his own race. Because of the time and
the place in which he grew up, Motley knew far less of the black
experience than did Wright, Baldwin, Himes, or Ellison. Growing
up in the 1920s, the only black literary figure he chose to emulate
was Alexandre Dumas, Père, whose picture he pasted inside the
cover of one of his clipping books containing his Bud Billiken columns. But it was authorship, not race, that gave Motley the strongest feeling of kinship with Dumas, and throughout his career he
devoted himself to writing about life as he actually knew it. His
writing of raceless novels at a time when they were enjoying a brief
vogue was less a piece of shrewd salesmanship than a historical
accident.

IV   *The Writer as Social Reformer*

Willard Motley earned a place in American literary history, perhaps in spite of the popular success that marked his works during

his lifetime. Uninterested in the technical advancement of the novel by stylistic innovations, he was nevertheless vitally interested in fiction that would speak to Americans and teach them something about areas of culture that they might have avoided in their daily lives. For Motley was not an "artist of the beautiful," but a novelist who, like many Naturalists, saw himself as a social reformer as well as a creative writer. By addressing the middle class, he could reach those people of his old neighborhood who had warned him about associating with the people he would find on Maxwell Street — those solid but myopic middle class citizens and the millions like them who shut the Nick Romanos away in reform schools and prisons and who ultimately called for their execution.

In spite of the fact that Motley will almost certainly never be ranked with the principal writers of the twentieth century, his honesty in revealing some of the city's hidden problems and his great sympathy in dealing with the youthful criminal, the narcotics addict, and the derelict should assure him a lasting niche in the history of the American novel.

Notes and References

Chapter One

1. See Robert E. Fleming, "Willard Motley's Date of Birth: An Error Corrected," *American Notes & Queries,* XIII, 1 (September 1974), 8–9. Although Motley's birth was not recorded by the Cook County Clerk, evidence exists in early issues of the Chicago *Defender* and in the author's diaries. See Motley's own column in the *Defender,* March 31, 1923, p. 14, col. 5, and references to his age in editors' notes appended to his stories and columns: *Defender,* September 23, 1922, p. 14, col. 6, and July 14, 1923, p. 14, col. 3. Diary entries for July 14, 1926, and July 14, 1930, refer to his seventeenth and twenty-first birthdays, respectively. Diaries are part of the Motley Collection, Parson Library, Northern Illinois University, hereafter cited as Northern Illinois Collection.
2. "Let No Man Write Epitaph of Hate for His Chicago," Chicago *Sunday Sun-Times,* August 11, 1963, sec. 2, p. 1, col. 3.
3. *Ibid.,* p. 1, col. 4; p. 2, col. 1.
4. *Ibid.,* p. 1, col. 4.
5. *Ibid.,* p. 2, col. 1.
6. Chicago *Defender,* September 23, 1922, p. 14, col. 6.
7. Chicago *Defender,* March 10, 1923, p. 14, col. 5.
8. "The Education of a Writer," *New Idea* (Winter 1961), p. 12.
9. Willard Motley to Archibald Motley, Sr., July 10, 1930, in the Northern Illinois Collection. See also diary entries June 29, 1930, to August 17, 1930.
10. "Education of a Writer," p. 12.
11. Undated sheet, Northern Illinois Collection.
12. "The Homecoming," five page carbon; "November Twenty-Second," 4 page typescript, Northern Illinois Collection.
13. Diary, January 1, 1941.
14. Typescript in Northern Illinois Collection.
15. Diary, January 1, 1941.
16. "Education of a Writer," p. 12.
17. " 'Religion' and the Handout," *Commonweal,* XXIX, 20 (March 10, 1939), 543.
18. "The Boy," *Ohio Motorist* (August 1938), pp. 14, 30–31; and "The Boy Grows Up," *Ohio Motorist* (May 1939), pages unknown. For the text of "The Boy," see Robert E. Fleming, "The First Nick Romano: the

Origins of *Knock on Any Door,"* *Mid America II* (East Lansing, Michigan; 1975), pp. 80–87.

19. Charles Wood, "The *Adventure* Manuscript: New Light on Willard Motley's Naturalism," *Negro American Literature Forum,* VI (Summer 1972), 35.

20. "Let No Man Write Epitaph of Hate for his Chicago," p. 3, col. 2.

21. "Pavement Portraits," *Hull-House Magazine,* I, 2 (December 1939), 2.

22. *Ibid.,* p. 4.

23. *Ibid.,* p. 6.

24. Typed supplement to diaries, Northern Illinois Collection.

25. Jack Conroy to Willard Motley, May 8, 1941, Northern Illinois Collection.

26. "The Beer Drinkers," p. 1. Typescript, Northern Illinois Collection.

27. *Ibid.,* p. 19.

28. "The Almost White Boy," in *Soon, One Morning,* Herbert Hill, ed. (New York, 1963), p. 400.

29. Diary, January 1, 1941.

30. *Ibid.*

31. Diary, July 14, 1941.

Chapter Two

1. Diary, March 10, 1941.

2. Undated note, Northern Illinois Collection.

3. Diary, May 8, 1941.

4. Diary, February 8, 1941.

5. Diary, April 22, 1941.

6. Diary, September 23, 1941.

7. Diary, October 27, 1941.

8. Diary, October 21, 1941.

9. "Little Sicily" manuscript [p. 15], Northern Illinois Collection.

10. Diary, October 8, 1942.

11. Diary, April 2, 1943.

12. Diary, March 20, 1943.

13. *Knock on Any Door* (New York, 1947), p. 474. Future references are cited parenthetically in the text.

14. Ray Brennan, "Best Seller Author Tells 8 Years' Work," Chicago *Daily Times,* May 24, 1947. Clipping in Motley's files, Northern Illinois Collection.

15. Jerome Klinkowitz and Karen Wood, "The Making and Unmaking of *Knock on Any Door,"* *Proof,* III (1973), 126.

16. *Ibid.*

17. *Ibid.,* p. 128.

18. *Ibid.*

19. *Ibid.,* p. 129.

20. *Ibid.,* p. 130.

21. See Clifford Shaw, *The Jack-Roller: A Delinquent Boy's Own Story* (Chicago, 1930); and Clifford Shaw and Maurice E. Moore, *The Natural History of a Delinquent Career* (Chicago, 1931).

22. Like Theodore Dreiser, who ameliorated the crimes of George Hurstwood and Clyde Griffiths, Motley was reluctant to attribute vicious impulses to his young criminal, who is attacked by society before he commits any serious offenses against it.

23. Klinkowitz and Wood, p. 126.

24. Blanche Houseman Gelfant, *The American City Novel* (Norman, Oklahoma; 1954), p. 185.

25. For a discussion of some of Motley's basic symbols, see Thomas D. Jarrett, "Sociology and Imagery in a Great American Novel," *English Journal,* XXXVIII (November 1949), 518–20.

26. Orville Prescott, "Books of the Times," New York *Times,* May 5, 1947, p. 21, cols. 2 and 3.

27. Margaret Hexter, "From Altar-Boy to Killer," *Saturday Review,* XXX, 21 (May 24, 1947), 13.

28. Phoebe Lou Adams, "Knock on Any Door," *Atlantic Monthly,* CLXXX, 1 (July 1947), 126–27.

29. Katherine Gauss Jackson, "Knock on Any Door," *Harper's Magazine,* CXCV (July 1947), [104].

30. Horace R. Cayton, "The Known City," *New Republic* (May 12, 1947), p. 31.

31. Horace R. Cayton, "A Terrifying Cross Section of Chicago," Chicago *Tribune,* May 4, 1947.

32. Horace R. Cayton, "Another Best-Seller by a Negro Is Not of the Negro or His Environs," Pittsburg *Courier,* May 24, 1947, p. 7, cols. 1, 2, and 3.

33. Arna Bontemps, "Chicago in Naturalistic Novel," New York *Herald Tribune Weekly Book Review,* May 18, 1947, VII, p. 8.

34. Philip Butcher, "In Print, The Literary Scene," *Opportunity,* XXV, 4 (Fall 1947), 218–22.

35. "America's Top Negro Authors," *Color,* V, 4 (June 1949), 28–31.

36. Jarrett, pp. 518–20.

37. Stanley Pargellis to Motley, May 14, 1947, Northern Illinois Collection.

38. Jarrett, p. 518.

39. Robert A. Bone, *The Negro Novel in America,* rev. ed. (New Haven, 1965), p. 179.

40. Alson Smith, *Chicago's Left Bank* (Chicago, 1953), p. 249.

41. Walter B. Rideout, *The Radical Novel in the United States: 1900-1954* (Cambridge, Mass., 1956), p. 288.

42. Gelfant, pp. 248–52.

Chapter Three

1. "Lonely Crusade," Chicago *Sun,* October 1, 1947, p. 33, col. 1.
2. *Ibid.,* col. 2.
3. The letters between Motley and Himes are reprinted in James Giles and Jerome Klinkowitz, "The Emergence of Willard Motley in Black American Literature," *Negro American Literature Forum,* VI (Summer 1972), 32; letter from Himes to Dedmon, Northern Illinois Collection.
4. Chester Himes, *The Quality of Hurt: The Autobiography of Chester Himes, I* (Garden City, N.Y.; 1972), p. 100.
5. Diary, December 12, 1941.
6. Typed carbon of Rosenwald application and outline of novel, Northern Illinois Collection.
7. Typed carbon of "One of the Family," Northern Illinois Collection.
8. Orville Prescott, "Books of the Times," New York *Times,* November 16, 1951, p. 23, cols. 2 and 3.
9. Frank Getlein, "We Fished All Night," *Commonweal,* LV (January 11, 1952), 357.
10. "The '30s Revisited," *Time* November 26, 1951, p. 122.
11. Harvey Swados, "Angry Novel," *Nation,* CLXXIII (December 29, 1951), 572.
12. James Gray, "Counsel of Despair," *Saturday Review,* XXXIV (December 8, 1951), 20–21.
13. Swados, p. 572.
14. Robert Cromie, "Motley's Cynical Study in Futility," Chicago *Tribune Magazine of Books,* November 25, 1951, pt. 4, p. 3.
15. Van Allen Bradley, "Books in the News," Chicago *Daily News,* November 21, 1951, p. 8.
16. *We Fished All Night* (New York, 1951), p. 517. Future references are cited parenthetically in text.
17. Since Motley told his editor, Ted Purdy of Appleton, that he did not want to harm the labor movement in his depiction of Norris, some of the strong prolabor scenes may have been intended to counter Norris's downfall. See Motley's letter to Purdy in Klinkowitz and Wood, p. 134.
18. William Dean Howells, *Criticism and Fiction* (New York, 1891), ch. II.
19. Bone, p. 180.
20. Thomas Wolfe, *Look Homeward Angel* (New York, 1929), ch. xxvii. In fact, Wolfe's use of an italicized epigraph that has biblical echoes and overtones suggests a possible source for Motley's idea of using such quotations, a device he used in no other works.
21. Nick Aaron Ford, "Four Popular Negro Novelists," *Phylon,* XV (1954), 34.

Chapter Four

1. Jack Conroy, "Typecasting an Author: Motley and the Novel that Never Got Written," Chicago *Daily News, Panorama,* February 26, 1966, p. 7, col. 2.
2. "The Return of Willard Motley," *Ebony,* XIII (December 1958), 88.
3. "The Education of a Writer," pp. 11–13, 15, 18, 20, 26, 28.
4. Motley to Hiram Haydn, February 26, 1958. Motley Collection, Memorial Library, University of Wisconsin. Hereafter cited as Wisconsin Collection.
5. See extracts from Motley to Haydn, February 28, 1958, in James R. Giles, "Willard Motley's Concept of 'Style' and 'Material,' " *Studies in Black Literature,* IV, 1 (Spring 1973), 4.
6. Motley to Hiram Haydn, February 28, 1958, Wisconsin Collection.
7. Klinkowitz and Wood, pp. 123–26.
8. See "The Education of a Writer"; "Let No Man Write Epitaph of Hate for His Chicago"; and Bob Ellison, "Three Best-Selling Authors: Conversations," *Rogue,* VIII, 6 (December 1963), 20, 22, 24, and 75.
9. *Let No Man Write My Epitaph* (New York, 1958), p. 16. Future references are cited parenthetically in the text.
10. Note dated October 23, 1962, in folder marked "Romanos," Wisconsin Collection.
11. David Dempsey, "Skid Row Revisited," New York *Times Book Review,* August 10, 1958, p. 18, cols. 2 and 3.
12. Nelson Algren, "Epitaph Writ in Syrup," *Nation,* CLXXXVII (August 16, 1958), 78.
13. "The Wire-Recorder Ear," *Time,* August 11, 1958, p. 74.
14. Granville Hicks, "Literary Horizons: Art and Reality," *Saturday Review,* XLI (August 9, 1958), 11.
15. Alfred Weissgarber, "Willard Motley and the Sociological Novel," *Studi Americani,* VII (1961), 307.
16. Diary, January 14, 1964 and January 15, 1965, Northern Illinois Collection.
17. Bone, p. 178.
18. *Knock on Any Door,* p. 149.

Chapter Five

1. Jack Conroy, p. 7, col. 1.
2. Motley's and Peter Israel's mutual disenchantment is documented by many letters in the Northern Illinois Collection: August and December 1962; April, May, June, October 1963; and June, August, September 1964. See also a folder of correspondence on *Let Noon Be Fair* in the Wisconsin Collection.
3. Motley to Israel, January 7, 1963, Northern Illinois Collection.

4. Motley to John Dodds, January 7, 1963, Wisconsin Collection.
5. Details on his poverty are from Motley's last journal covering November 6, 1961, to February 19, 1965, about two weeks before his death. Northern Illinois Collection.
6. Motley to Israel, April 25, 1963, Northern Illinois Collection.
7. Robert H. Donahugh, "Let Noon Be Fair," *Library Journal,* XCI (February 1, 1966), 715.
8. Conroy, p. 7, col. 2.
9. Charles Poore, "The Death and Life of a Tropic Town," New York *Times,* February 24, 1966, sec. C, p. 39, col. 4.
10. Alexander Coleman, "All the Farther for Being Near," New York *Times Book Review,* February 27, 1966, p. 42, col. 5.
11. Jose Donoso, "From Heaven to Hilton: Willard Motley's *Let Noon Be Fair,*" *Saturday Review,* XLIX (March 12, 1966), 152.
12. Nelson Algren, "The Trouble at Gringo Gulch," *Book Week,* March 6, 1966, pp. 5, 15.
13. *Let Noon Be Fair* (New York, 1966), p. 279. Future references are cited parenthetically in the text.
14. Motley to Israel, April, 25, 1963, Northern Illinois Collection.

Chapter Six

1. "The Return of Willard Motley," pp. 84–88, 90.
2. Mavis McIntosh to Motley, May 5, 1960. Wisconsin Collection.
3. The entire Motley-Loomis correspondence on "My House Is Your House" (June 1959 to July 1961) is in the Wisconsin Collection. See especially Loomis to Motley, March 13, 1961.
4. "A Kilo of Tortillas, A Güaje of Pulque," *Rogue,* IX, 4 (August 1964), 48.
5. *Ibid.,* p. 57.
6. "Give the Gentleman What He Wants," *Rogue,* IX, 5 (October 1964), 16. Italics are Motley's.
7. *Ibid.*
8. "Death Leaves a Candle," *Rogue,* X, 4 (August 1965), 21.
9. Motley to Elizabeth McKee, July 22, 1960, Wisconsin Collection.
10. Elizabeth McKee to Motley, February 13, 1962, February 21, 1962, February 27, 1962, Wisconsin Collection.
11. Motley to Elizabeth McKee, February 23, 1962, February 24, 1962, Wisconsin Collection.
12. Klinkowitz and Wood, p. 134.
13. *Ibid.,* pp. 135–36.
14. "The Almost White Boy," pp. 389–400.
15. Giles, p. 5.
16. The Wisconsin Collection contains five letters from Hughes to Motley and carbons of two letters from Motley to Hughes.

17. The Wisconsin Collection contains three letters from Petry to Motley; one carbon from Motley to Petry.

18. The Wisconsin Collection contains two letters from Brown to Motley; one carbon from Motley to Brown. One of the former letters is published in Giles and Klinkowitz, p. 34.

19. Motley to Frederica Westbrooke, October 7, 1961, Wisconsin Collection.

20. "Stand Up and Be Counted," *Time,* LXXXI, 23 (June 7, 1963), 11. The Baldwin story was published in *Time,* LXXXI, 20 (May 17, 1963), 26–27.

21. "Let No Man Write Epitaph of Hate for His Chicago," sec. 2, pp. 1–4.

22. *Ibid.,* p. 1.

23. *Ibid.*

24. *Ibid.,* p. 4.

25. See "The Return of Willard Motley."

26. "Willard Motley Dies in Mexico; Author of 'Knock on Any Door,' " New York *Times,* March 5, 1965, p. 30, col. 1.

Chapter Seven

1. Bone, p. 179.

2. *Ibid.,* p. 180.

3. Gelfant, p. 249.

4. Harvey Breit, "James Baldwin and Two Footnotes," *The Creative Present: Notes on Contemporary American Fiction,* eds. Nona Balakian and Charles Simmons (Garden City, N.Y.; 1963), pp. 21–22.

5. John F. Bayliss, "Nick Romano: Father and Son," *Negro American Literature Forum,* III, 1 (Spring 1969), 21.

6. Bone, p. 178.

7. *Ibid.,* p. 168. See also pp. 169–72, 178–85, on the raceless novel.

8. Charles I. Glicksberg, "The Alienation of Negro Literature," *Phylon,* XI (First Quarter 1950), 49.

9. See also John S. Lash, "The Race Consciousness of the American Negro Author," *Social Forces,* XXVIII (October 1949), 24–34, which concluded that racial subject matter had been a limiting factor for black authors.

10. Thomas D. Jarrett, "Toward Unfettered Creativity: A Note on the Negro Novelist's Coming of Age," *Phylon,* XI (Fourth Quarter 1950), 315.

11. *Ibid.,* p. 316.

12. The integrationist point of view was opposed by another faction during this period. See Nick Aaron Ford, "A Blueprint for Negro Authors," *Phylon,* XI (Fourth Quarter 1950), 374–77; and Lloyd L. Brown, "Which Way for the Negro Writer?" *Masses and Mainstream,* IV

(March 1951), 53–63; (April 1951), 50–59.
   13. Michel Fabre, *The Unfinished Quest of Richard Wright* (New York, 1973), p. 381.

Selected Bibliography

PRIMARY SOURCES

1. Books

Knock on Any Door. New York: D. Appleton-Century, 1947.
We Fished All Night. New York: Appleton-Century-Crofts, 1951.
Let No Man Write My Epitaph. New York: Random House, 1958.
Let Noon Be Fair. New York: G. P. Putnam's Sons, 1966.
The Diaries of Willard Motley. Edited by Jerome Klinkowitz. Ames, Iowa: The Iowa State University Press. Forthcoming.

2. Contributions to Periodicals

"The Boy." *Ohio Motorist* (August 1938), pp. 14, 30–31.
"Calle Olvera — America's Most Picturesque Street." *The Highway Traveler,* X (August-September 1938), 14–15, 41–46.
" 'Religion' and the Handout." *Commonweal,* XXIX, 20 (March 10, 1939), 542–43.
"Assault on Catalina." *Outdoors,* VII (April 1939), 30–31.
"The Boy Grows Up." *Ohio Motorist* (May 1939), pages unknown.
"Small Town Los Angeles." *Commonweal,* XXX (June 30, 1939), 251–52.
"Idaho Presents Shoshone Falls." *Automobile and Trailer Travel Magazine,* IV (August 1939), 14–15.
"Hull-House Neighborhood." *Hull-House Magazine,* I, 1 (November 1939), 5–7.
"Pavement Portraits." *Hull-House Magazine,* I, 2 (December 1939), 2–6.
"Handfuls." *Hull-House Magazine,* I, 3 (January 1940), 9–11.
"Negro Art in Chicago." *Opportunity,* XVIII (January 1940), 19–22, 28–31.
"We Climb Mount Hood." *Ohio Motorist* (April 1940), pp. 12–13, 18.
"Who Made This Boy a Murderer?" (excerpts from *Knock on Any Door*). *Look,* XI (September 30, 1947), 21–31.
"Lonely Crusade" (review). Chicago *Sun,* October 1, 1947, p. 33, cols. 1 and 2.
"Knock on Any Door" (abridgement; featured on cover). *Omnibook Magazine,* IX (October 1947), [1]–46.
"The Education of a Writer" (transcript of a lecture). *New Idea* (Winter 1961), pp. 11–13, 15, 18, 20, 26, 28.
"Let No Man Write Epitaph of Hate for His Chicago." Chicago *Sunday Sun-Times,* August 11, 1963, sec. 2, pp. 1–4.

"The Almost White Boy." In *Soon, One Morning,* ed. Herbert Hill, pp. 389–400. New York: Alfred A. Knopf, 1963.
"A Kilo of Tortillas, A Güaje of Pulque." *Rogue,* IX, 4 (August, 1964), 46–48, 57.
"Give the Gentleman What He Wants." *Rogue,* IX, 5 (October 1964), 14–16, 75.
"Christmas in Mexico." *Rogue,* IX, 6 (December 1964), pages unknown.
"Death Leaves a Candle." *Rogue,* X, 4 (August 1965), 19–22, 79.

3. Manuscript Materials

Motley Collection, Swen Franklin Parson Library, Northern Illinois University, DeKalb, Illinois: Large collection of letters, notes, clippings, journals, and early manuscripts of *Knock on Any Door, We Fished All Night, Let Noon Be Fair,* and a number of unpublished manuscripts, including "My House Is Your House." Loaned by the Estate of Willard Motley.
Motley Collection, Memorial Library, University of Wisconsin, Madison, Wisconsin: Letters, notes, clippings, and some manuscripts. Donated by Motley.
James Weldon Johnson Memorial Collection, Beinecke Rare Book and Manuscript Library, Yale University Library, New Haven, Connecticut: Typescript of *Knock on Any Door* (missing first 87 pages; total of 1078 pages). Donated by Motley.

SECONDARY SOURCES

"America's Top Negro Authors." *Color,* V (June 1949), 28–31. About the popularity of Motley, Richard Wright, W. E. B. DuBois, Ann Petry, and Langston Hughes,
BAYLISS, JOHN F. "Nick Romano: Father and Son." *Negro American Literature Forum,* III, 1 (Spring 1969), 18–21, 32. Thematic and stylistic connections between *Knock on Any Door* and *Let No Man Write My Epitaph.*
BONE, ROBERT A. *The Negro Novel in America.* Revised edition. New Haven and London: Yale University Press, 1965. *Knock on Any Door* and *We Fished All Night* as "raceless novels."
BONTEMPS, ARNA. "Famous WPA Authors." *Negro Digest,* VIII (June 1950), 43–47. Influence of the Works Progress Administration Writers' Projects on Chicago's black writers, including Motley.
BREIT, HARVEY. "James Baldwin and Two Footnotes." In *The Creative Present: Notes on Contemporary American Fiction,* eds., Nona Balakian and Charles Simmons. Garden City, New York: Doubleday & Co., 1963. Praises Motley's portrayal of white characters and the tragedy of life.

EISINGER, CHESTER E. *Fiction of the Forties.* Chicago: University of Chicago Press, 1963. Compares *Knock on Any Door* with Ann Petry's *The Street* (1946).

ELLISON, BOB. "Three Best-Selling Authors: Conversations." *Rogue,* VIII, 6 (December 1963), 20, 22, 24, and 75. Interviews with Motley, Harper Lee, and Nelson Algren.

FLEMING, ROBERT E. "Willard Motley's Urban Novels." *Umoja: South-western Afro-American Journal,* I (Summer 1973), 15–19. Motley as critic of the American city; emphasizes treatment of juvenile delinquency, narcotics addiction, organized labor, and politics.

———. Willard Motley's Date of Birth: An Error Corrected." *American Notes & Queries,* XIII, 1 (September 1974), 8–9. Establishes Motley's birth date as July 14, 1909.

———. "The First Nick Romano: The Origins of *Knock on Any Door.*" In *Mid America II,* ed. David D. Anderson, pp. 80.–87. East Lansing, Michigan: Midwestern Press, 1975. Discussion and reprinting of "The Boy."

FORD, NICK AARON. "Four Popular Negro Novelists." *Phylon,* XV (1954), 29–39. Comparison of Wright, Frank Yerby, Motley, and Ralph Ellison.

GELFANT, BLANCHE HOUSEMAN. *The American City Novel.* Norman: University of Oklahoma Press, 1954. *Knock on Any Door* as a modern counterpart of Dreiser's *An American Tragedy.* Motley's works compared and contrasted with those of Nelson Algren.

GILES, JAMES R. "Willard Motley's Concept of 'Style' and 'Material': Some Comments Based Upon the Motley Collection at the University of Wisconsin." *Studies in Black Literature,* IV, 1 (Spring 1973), 4–6. Motley's correspondence with his editors and its bearing on his literary theories.

GILES, JAMES R. and JEROME KLINKOWITZ. "The Emergence of Willard Motley in Black American Literature." *Negro American Literature Forum,* VI, 2 (Summer 1972), 31–34. Quotes from and reproduces selected letters fromMotley's papers to document his relationship with other black writers. This issue also contains five photographs of the South Side of Chicago, taken by Motley for the Federal Writers' Project (pp. 38, 45, 51).

GILES, JAMES R. and N. JILL WEYANT. "The Short Fiction of Willard Motley." *Negro American Literature Forum,* IX, 1 (Spring 1975), 3–10. Motley's unpublished stories in the Northern Illinois University Collection.

GRENANDER, M. E. "Criminal Responsibility in *Native Son* and *Knock on Any Door.*" *American Literature,* XLIX (May 1977), [221]-33. Treats the environmentalist theory underlying both novels.

HOFFMAN, F. J. *The Modern Novel in America: 1900–1950.* Chicago: Henry Regnery Company, 1951. *Knock on Any Door* and Nelson

Algren's *The Man With the Golden Arm* (1949) as treatments of the skid row subculture.

HUGHES, CARL MILTON. *The Negro Novelist: A Discussion of the Writings of American Negro Novelists, 1940–1950.* New York: The Citadel Press, 1953. *Knock on Any Door* and *We Fished All Night* as works from the universal school of black writers.

JARRETT, THOMAS D. "Sociology and Imagery in a Great American Novel." *English Journal,* XXXVIII (November 1949), 518–20. The relationship between Motley's deterministic philosophy and the imagery employed in *Knock on Any Door.*

KLINKOWITZ, JEROME; JAMES GILES; and JOHN T. O'BRIEN. "The Willard Motley Papers at the University of Wisconsin." *Resources for American Literary Study,* II (Autumn 1972), 218–73. A catalogue of the correspondence, notes, and manuscripts (most dating from 1957–1963) in the collection.

KLINKOWITZ, JEROME, and KAREN WOOD. "The Making and Unmaking of *Knock on Any Door.*" *Proof,* III (1973), 121–37. Motley's problems in revising his first novel. Includes hitherto unpublished preface to *Knock on Any Door* and correspondence with editor.

MAJOR, CLARENCE. *The Dark and Feeling: Black American Writers and Their Work.* New York: Third Press, 1974. Personal reminiscences of a meeting with Motley and comments about his work.

————. "Open Letters: A Column." *The American Poetry Review,* V (October–November 1975), 22. Outlines some of Motley's concerns expressed in his diaries.

RAYSON, ANN L. "Prototypes for Nick Romano of *Knock on Any Door.*" *Negro American Literature Forum,* VIII, 3 (Fall 1974), 248–51. Genesis of Nick Romano as seen in unpublished short stories written before *Knock on Any Door.*

"The Return of Willard Motley." *Ebony,* XIII (December 1958), 84–88, 90. Motley's comments on Chicago and on why he chose to live in Mexico.

RIDEOUT, WALTER B. *The Radical Novel in the United States: 1900–1954.* Cambridge: Harvard University Press, 1956. Treats both *Knock on Any Door* and *We Fished All Night* from a political point of view.

SCHRAUFNAGEL, NOEL. *From Apology to Protest: The Black American Novel.* Deland, Fla.: Everett Edwards, Inc., 1973. Brief discussion of Motley, mostly *Knock on Any Door,* as part of nonracial protest movement of the 1940s.

WEISSGARBER, ALFRED. "Willard Motley and the Sociological Novel." *Studi Americani,* VII (1961), 299–309. Considers Motley as a social reformer first and an artist second.

WEYANT, N. JILL. "Lyrical Experimentation in Willard Motley's Mexican Novel: *Let Noon Be Fair.*" *Negro American Literature Forum,* X, 1 (Spring 1976), 95–99. Discusses Motley's departure from his earlier

Naturalistic techniques in his final novel.

———. "Willard Motley's Pivotal Novel: *Let No Man Write My Epitaph.*" *Black American Literature Forum,* XI, 2 (Summer 1977), 56–61. Considers *Epitaph* significant because it marked Motley's acceptance of his blackness and prepared him to write a technically superior novel, *Let Noon Be Fair.*

WOOD, CHARLES. "The *Adventure* Manuscript: New Light on Willard Motley's Naturalism." *Negro American Literature Forum,* VI, 2 (Summer 1972), 35–38. Description and discussion of Motley's book length manuscript on his two trips west.

Index